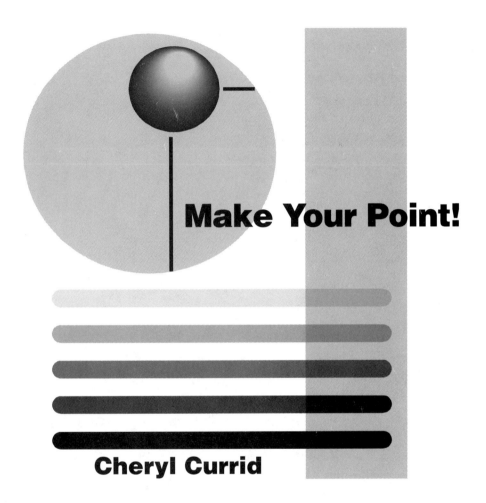

Make Your Point!

Cheryl Currid

PRIMA PUBLISHING
Rocklin, California

Managing Editor: Paula Munier Lee

Acquisitions Editor: Sherri Morningstar

Project Editor: Stefan Grünwedel

Cover Production Coordinator: Anne Flemke

Copy Editor: Vivian Jaquette

Emergency Fact Checker: Arline Sabia

Book Design and Production: Susan Glinert, BookMakers

Indexer: Brown Editorial Service

Cover Designer: Page Design, Inc.

Prima Publishing and the author have attempted throughout this book to distinguish proprietary trademarks from descriptive terms by following the capitalization style used by the manufacturer.

Information contained in this book has been obtained by Prima Publishing from sources believed to be reliable. However, because of the possibility of human or mechanical error by our sources, Prima Publishing, or others, the Publisher does not guarantee the accuracy, adequacy, or completeness of any information and is not responsible for any errors or omissions or the results obtained from use of such information.

ISBN: 1-55958-414-9

Library of Congress Catalog Card Number: 93-34367

Printed in the United States of America

95 96 97 98 RRD 10 9 8 7 6 5 4 3 2 1

To my mother, Evelyn Clarke,
for her unfailing encouragement.

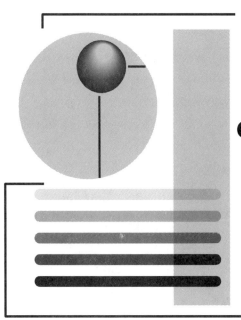

Contents

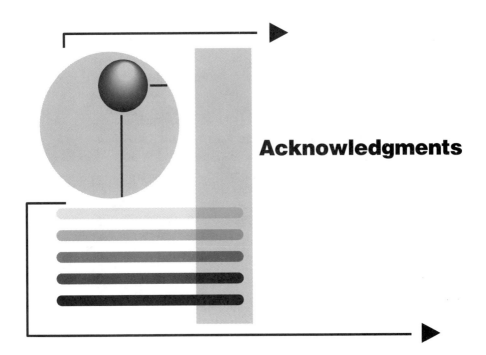

Acknowledgments

Producing a book isn't too different from producing a play. There are always many more people contributing from behind the curtain than who set foot on stage. In this work, I am grateful for the efforts of several key players.

Thanks must first go to my professional colleague, sidekick, and friend, Diane Bolin. Through thick and thin, as well as nearly a dozen books, Diane has patiently waded through many manuscripts and offered first-line support for moving projects along. I feel truly honored to have had her enduring support for this and other Currid & Company books. Diane knows her stuff, respects deadlines, and makes sure others do too. For this work she undertook an accelerated role and even helped smooth out the rough edges. If anyone were to hand out an award for MVP for this project, she'd certainly get it.

I'd also like to acknowledge the efforts of Debbie Richards and Bill Pearson, who both contributed significantly to the early manuscript formation. Debbie's experience, spanning over a decade in professional design, graphics, and multimedia certainly helped add special insight to little known tips, tricks, and techniques. Bill's long-time experience in event planning and professional radio and TV appearances help give readers even more insight into putting everything together.

Finally, let me extend my heartfelt thanks to this book's project editor at Prima Publishing, Stefan Grünwedel. This book marks our fourth project together. I've grown to respect his judgment and excellent sense of what's right for the printed word. Stefan hasn't taught me all the tricks of being a good writer yet, but he sure has shown me many.

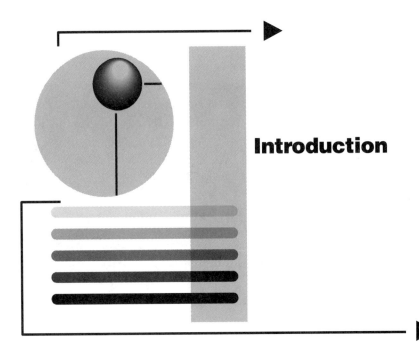

Introduction

If you've ever wanted to improve your business communication skills, you've come to the right place. This book is directed, focused, and even fixated on helping businesspeople develop better business presentations. Plain and simple. I show my bias about using low-cost technology to spruce up those presentations.

After all, success in business today doesn't happen by chance, and successful lectures are no accident. People don't just show up, set up, and make stunning, informative business presentations; they must work at it and use all the tricks available to them.

The rewards are worth it. For some, getting the point across means sheer survival in the business jungle. The career progression of many business professionals, salespeople, and other savvy workers depends on their ability to pull together information from a wide variety of sources and then give clear, concise, and informative presentations. The stakes can be high.

WHY YOU NEED THIS BOOK

Whether you are trying to convince someone to approve a budget, make a billion-dollar investment, or try out a new product, chances are you've got your credibility and professional reputation on the line. Whether you speak to an audience of 5 or 5,000 people, this book can help you prepare, organize, and deliver a great message. It combines the wisdom you'd gain from a course on presentation style with the benefits you'd get from learning a lot about computer tools. It goes beyond the typical tutorials for using software and hardware by giving you valuable tips and tricks that will help you deliver your message and make your point.

I believe that putting together effective business presentations is now easier than ever. I've studied the tools, techniques, and technologies for a long time. With a little work, almost anybody can become an effective presenter; it just takes focus, organization, and the right tools.

In today's world of information overload, you as a business presenter must rally all the forces and sources you can. Generally, the forces come from within—they come from your conviction and belief in what you are talking about. The sources are what you use to make sure your audience takes in your message, whether they are research figures, quotes, or stunning audiovisual displays.

The Not-so-Good Old Days

Making business presentations has changed a lot over the years. Until recently, only the most well-paid, high-ranking, or creative people could put together powerful presentations. They also needed an army of support people to help out. The troops included speechwriters, research assistants, graphic artists, storyboard editors, paste-up artists, secretaries, proofreaders, and various other production helpers.

Even when computers first entered the scene, the process didn't get much easier. Early computer gear was very specialized and required trained operators. Art methods, too, were slow, labor-intensive, and expensive. A single text slide could cost over $200 to produce. Last-minute changes were nearly impossible to accommodate.

So much for the old days. Today, with low-cost, high-tech tools, many of the old jobs can be rolled into one, and it's easy to create razzle-dazzle effects. Today's technology lets you embed sound and video into your presentations almost as easily as you enter a line of text into your word processor.

Putting High-Tech Tools to Work

Technology changes all the rules, even the rules about who does what. In many business situations, the preparer is also the presenter—as well as the proofreader, art director, and production helper. Even for large meetings and major presentations, the production staff can often be reduced to a few key people.

Today's business presenter might wear some or all of the hats. If that person turns out to be you, then you've been given a great opportunity. Chances are that you will achieve better control of content and quality—that is, if you use the right techniques.

That's what *Make Your Point!* is all about. I want to share with you how much technology can help you. No, computers won't make you a wonderful business presenter. They won't stop your knees from knocking the first few times you walk on stage. But computers and related technology will help you in many other ways. They will help you organize your thoughts, research your topic, and prepare your text and graphics. Technology can also serve as a silent coach and help you rehearse. Moreover, if you choose to bring your computer along, it can add some memorable effects to your presentation.

Building a Great Presentation Step by Step

In the pages that follow you'll get a quick course in building and delivering business presentations—from beginning to end. I have organized this book to follow the process in four parts: preparing, producing, presenting, and postmortem analysis. Each part contains a number of chapters that help you through the sequence of activities. The last part also takes you through an example of an outstanding presentation.

Part I, "Preparing," discusses the activities you need to do to get started. I start with a little philosophy about giving business presentations and why they're important. Then I turn to the mechanics of getting prepared. I talk about organizing your schedule, your outline, and your research.

Part II, "Producing," covers the ins and outs of putting presentations together. I cover the mechanics of how to work with presentation-support software and how to build a presentation toolbox.

Part III, "Presenting," turns your attention to the special style and techniques that you'll need to deliver a polished presentation.

Part IV, "Postmortem and Putting It All Together," considers how you might do the job just a little better next time. Becoming a good presenter takes more than practice; it takes constructive criticism and a constant search for better presentation techniques. I also show you how to develop a 20-minute presentation from beginning to end, using all the skills discussed in this book.

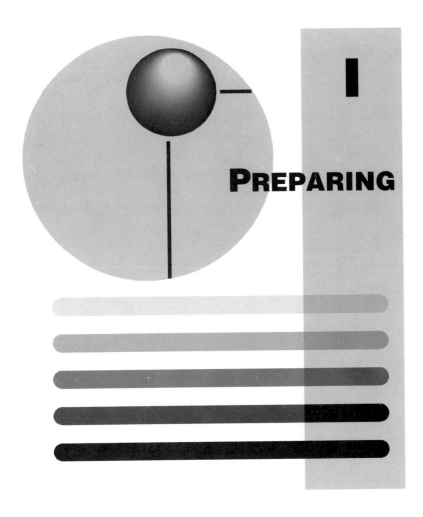

PREPARING

Name your challenge. You have been asked to give a presentation to the board of directors to justify a new million-dollar project. Your professional organization wants you to speak to members about the state of your industry. Your organization is undergoing major upheaval and you must present the company strategy to your staff. It is your responsibility to communicate or convince your audience of something. What do you do first? How do you make the most effective presentation? How do you develop a plan? What is the real message you want to tell them? Quick, grab this book and read Part I. It gets you started on the right foot.

Part I of *Make Your Point!* helps you lay out your plan. I spend a lot of time covering the basics of presentations, and how to develop the message—what you *really* want to tell 'em.

I also introduce technology to help you be organized and communicate your message. New hardware and software, complete with powerful portable computers and a growing list of dynamic and powerful presentation software, enable you to craft your message in the best, most innovative, and exciting manner possible. When you combine what you have to say with the power tools—exciting, dynamic, innovative presentation software—you will succeed as never before!

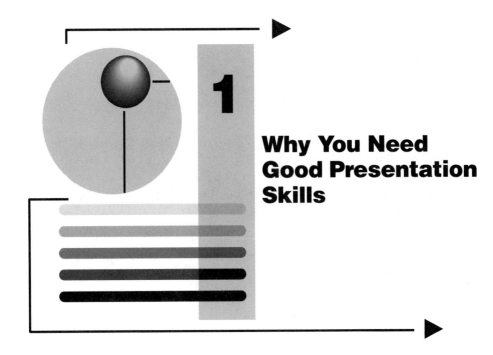

Why You Need Good Presentation Skills

"You can have brilliant ideas, but if you can't get them across, your brains won't get you anywhere. I've known a lot of engineers with terrific ideas who had trouble explaining them to other people. It's always a shame when a guy with great talent can't tell the board or a committee what's in his head."

Lee Iacocca, *An Autobiography*

For most of us, business today requires effective communications skills. No matter what the job—private sector, government agency, small business or large—every businessperson must contribute knowledge to their organization. Often, that contribution requires some form of business presentation.

And, as 21st-century business styles emerge, look for some important trends to escalate. People will need to make business decisions faster and issues will grow more complex. It will become more important for people to be good communicators and to learn how to use every trick in the book to get their messages across.

After all, in a society saturated with information, it's easy to get lost in all the noise. Getting a message through can be a complex affair. Often, communicating your message requires that you engage as many of your audience's senses as possible.

Don't just write a report: *Tell* them. Show them a picture. Make an impression. Get them involved.

Of course, I don't suggest that you give up all efforts to produce books and reports, and then head for Hollywood. There will always be a need to communicate certain details and backup information in simple, written form. But I strongly believe that the days of presenting your message in a monotone voice or with plainly typed text are long gone.

More than ever, businesspeople who have to communicate a message, thought, or idea must activate the audience's senses. Colorful visuals, motion, and multiple sounds all help capture the audience's attention and imagination.

No doubt you've seen the statistics. People retain more information when they see it, hear it, and get involved with it. Over the years, different studies have shown that retention rates more than double when people see as well as hear the information presented.

The old adage "a picture is worth a thousand words" holds as true in business today as ever. Adding visuals to a presentation can reduce the time required to grasp a concept by up to 40 percent, according to Bert Decker, leader of the successful consulting firm Decker Communications, Inc.

Picture versus words

He can leap tall buildings in a single bound.

THE PRESENTER'S PARADOX

Most people in business have long recognized the importance of communication skills. A *Journal of Business Communication* survey of business leaders revealed these findings:

▶ 62 percent of businesspeople said the ability to write well was very important to their jobs.

▶ 90 percent said the ability to speak well was very important.

The National Research Bureau reported the results of a survey of career skills required for the upwardly mobile career professional. Topping the list of desired skills was the ability to communicate ideas and plans in front of an audience. In fact, presentation skills ranked far higher than selling, negotiation, and persuasive talents. Moreover, 75 percent of the executives surveyed in this study said that presentation skills are three times more important for career advancement than is writing aptitude.

Experts estimate that over 30 million business presentations take place every day. Delivering presentations has become a routine task for many business professionals. In fact, half of the business professionals polled in one survey said they took to the podium at least once a month.

Fear of Public Speaking

While these figures are impressive, they fail to show the dark side of giving business presentations: "oratophobia," or fear of speaking in public. Many businesspeople suffer from stage fright.

According to a poll published by the *San Francisco Chronicle,* when people were asked to list their greatest fear, most responded with "speaking in front of a large group of people." It ranked higher than fear of death. In a research-firm study, R.H. Bruskin reported that 40 percent of adults cited public speaking as their number-one fear. The *Book of Lists,* which surveyed 3,000 people about what they feared, placed "speaking" on top of the list of fears—ahead of fear of heights, bugs, and death.

Frightened Man & Woman

So the "presentation paradox" confronts many people, and maybe even you: You know that delivering an effective business presentation is good for your career, but you are scared to death of speaking in front of people.

Rising Audience Expectations

As if the pressures of public speaking weren't enough, now consider them in today's business world. These days it's not enough to simply organize well, write well, or speak well. Business presenters must learn how to "edutain" their audiences.

After all, look who is showing up in the business audience—the MTV generation! A whole generation of people who cut their teeth on "edutainment" have descended on corporations. As youngsters they were schooled by "Sesame Street," then they graduated to music videos, and now they refer to CD-ROM–based multimedia encyclopedias. At almost every stage, people now expect to learn from multiple sources.

And that expectation travels right from the home to the office. Often, today's businesspeople want their business information presented as colorfully as their entertainment.

Of course, this represents a new challenge to business presenters. It's not enough to simply broadcast a message on one channel—like written text, or speech only. Presenters must transmit the message over multiple channels, appealing to multiple senses.

WHAT CAN YOU ACCOMPLISH WITH SUCCESSFUL PRESENTATIONS?

As business becomes increasingly complex, there is a growing need to increase the clarity of all communication. We must include in our bag of professional tools the ability to present information understandably—and on multiple channels. Everyone must develop the skills to sell their ideas, often through face-to-face presentations.

With successful presentations, you can accomplish all of the following:

▶ Keep management informed on project or program status; improve decision-making

▶ Keep employees involved and informed on company or department direction and focus; enhance morale and company culture

▶ Communicate information among peers; enhance knowledge of every individual on the team

▶ Sell the company's products or services; grow the business

▶ Sell the company's vision; encourage investment in the business

▶ Sell yourself; grow your career

Conveying Your Winning Ideas

Remember the old riddle, "If a tree falls in the forest and no one is there to hear it, does it still make a noise?" Perhaps I can twist that question a little and ask, "If the most brilliant idea surfaces in someone's mind, but it does not get out, is it still a brilliant idea?"

Probably not. Chances are, even the most marvelous idea is worth very little until it goes from one person to another. Whether an audience accepts and understands your ideas may very well depend upon how you communicate them.

It's possible that some of the greatest ideas ever conceived never left the brain of the creator and that many of the greatest ideas ever communicated went unrecognized. Unfortunately, none of these ideas did anyone any good.

Taking Responsibility

A very wise founder and CEO of a Fortune 100 company asked his employees, "If you and I share what we know with each other, we will both make better decisions. Now how can we grow that concept throughout this company so that we as a company can then make the best decisions possible?"

The idea makes sense, but to implement it would represent a big challenge. Such a program would require that businesses help every employee improve his or her communication capabilities. Since companies are unlikely to fund such training for everyone, perhaps the individuals themselves should take responsibility for their development in this area. Reading and practicing the concepts presented in this book could be a very good start.

Planning for Success

If I had to summarize the key success factors for today's business professional, I would be sure to include the tips, tricks, techniques, and technologies for making effective presentations. These aren't the only skills you'll need to become successful, but they certainly are important ones.

As you progress through the following chapters of this book, you will see how I have set up the road map for giving effective business presentations. You will get suggestions and checklists at each step along the way.

Depending on your specific assignment, you will want to adjust and fine-tune your planning and activities. I don't expect you to spend two months full-time in preparations for a 15-minute update presentation to your workgroup colleagues. On the other hand, you should give more than a passing thought to a 45-minute speech if you have been invited to deliver a presentation to both houses of Congress.

I'll note where you can bring in technology to help you along. Whether it's a simple $29 tape recorder or elaborate computer gear, I'll be sure to point out how today's technology can make your presentation go more smoothly.

And now on to the first phase. As I mentioned in the introduction, delivering a presentation can be broken into four phases: preparing, producing, presenting, and postmortem. Let's start now with preparing.

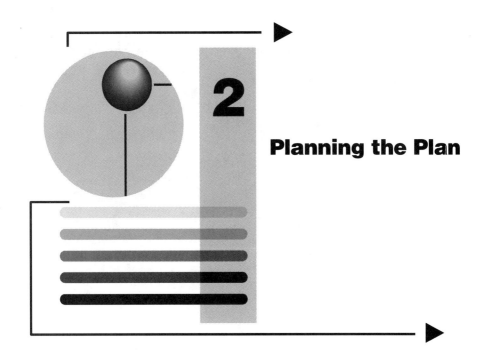

Planning the Plan

So, you're about to give a business presentation? Good. Whether you are a novice presenter or an expert, getting ready to speak before a small audience or a large group, remember one key phrase:

"Proper planning prevents poor performance."

Everyone who gives a presentation should heed those words. In today's fast-paced world, businesspeople expect high-impact presentations. Often, the audience wants and needs lots of information summarized and delivered quickly and effectively.

The only way a presenter can fill the needs of an audience is to prepare thoroughly and carefully. Experts in the field of presentations say that for every minute of presentation, the presenter needs to spend one to five hours preparing. Sounds like a lot, doesn't it? Table 2-1 shows how the recommended preparation time varies depending on your knowledge of the topic and the resources available to you.

Table 2-1 Time Required for Each Minute of Presentation

Hours of Preparation	Personal Knowledge of Topic	Access to Electronic Template	Access to Electronic Research
5	Minimal	No	No
4.5	Minimal	Yes	No
4	Minimal	Yes	Yes
3.5	Moderate	No	No
3.5	Moderate	Yes	No
3	Moderate	Yes	Yes
2.5	Extensive	No	No
2	Extensive	Yes	No
1-1.5	Extensive	Yes	Yes

Of course, you'll save preparation time if you are simply updating a presentation you created previously. I know professional speakers who deliver the same basic presentation time after time, with only slight changes for the audience. In these cases, the presenter may spend as little as 10 to 20 minutes preparing for each minute of presentation.

Also, your own expertise and access to good research tools can help you cut your preparation time while developing a comprehensive presentation. I find that electronic presentation templates and electronic databases for research are especially useful.

In this chapter I take a look at the planning process for creating a practically perfect presentation. (I say "practically" because there is no such thing as a perfect presentation.) I introduce three early steps in planning your presentation: accepting the assignment, getting started, and developing an action plan. By following each step, you'll get off to a great start.

ACCEPTING THE ASSIGNMENT

Whether you've been asked to speak at the next workgroup status meeting or you just opened an invitation to address a group of 5,000, your first step is to accept the assignment. Note that I say "accept," because in most business situations, you do have an opportunity to accept or decline the invitation.

No Thanks, I'm Busy

There are plenty of excuses for declining a speaking invitation: You don't have time, you don't know enough about the topic, you'd rather have your boss do it, you'd rather have a colleague do it, you need a haircut—the list goes on. As I discussed in Chapter 1, the fear of public speaking is widespread, and some people will do anything to avoid it.

Before you mail off your regrets, however, keep in mind that refusing an invitation to speak will get you off the hook, but you might be missing out on a great opportunity. Presentation skills can contribute greatly to career advancement.

So if you find yourself looking down the list of excuses to decline your next speaking invitation, be sure to consider the consequences. Don't gripe if someone else takes the opportunity and then enhances his or her position in the workgroup, company, or industry.

About the only legitimate reason to turn down a speaking invitation is if you really don't have time to prepare. If you can't somehow squeeze a few extra hours from your evenings or weekends, then it's okay to decline. You are better off declining than giving an unpolished performance that could hurt your credibility.

But if the only thing keeping you from presenting is stage fright, I recommend taking a public-speaking class or joining a club such as Toastmasters. You'll soon gain the confidence you need to speak in front of groups—and then you can spend your time preparing instead of looking for excuses.

Yes, I'll Do It!

Giving a presentation to any group gives you a chance to tell them what you know. It also gives you an opportunity to sharpen your knowledge. You may think you already know a lot about a given topic, but if you have to give a presentation, you'll undoubtedly become an expert. There's an old saying: "If you really want to learn something, teach it."

Of course, delivering a good presentation has other benefits. It gives you a chance to impress, inform, and persuade people. So for most speaking invitations, the best reply is an unqualified yes.

GETTING STARTED

From the moment you accept a speaking engagement, you should begin developing your plan and schedule. You need to mobilize your forces quickly and get a plan going. You can start by getting answers to five basic questions that will get you mentally prepared for the presentation. Create a document in your word-processing program and type in the following headings for the first five things you need to research:

▶ What
▶ Why
▶ Who
▶ When
▶ Where

For some experienced presenters, seeking answers to "the five W's" might seem a little bit like elementary school. The answers, however, form the basic building blocks for your presentation. Answering them can help you quickly size up the needs of your presentation and avoid overlooked details and "gotchas." Come back to these questions throughout the preparation process to make sure you're staying on track.

What

The most important question to answer is *What*. What topic are you expected to speak about? What kind of message about that topic will you deliver?

Defining the topic is usually an easy process. Your boss will ask you to talk about your company's market position, its newest product or service, or its latest fumble. The information you deliver can be good news or bad. You may need to convince your audience to take action, or perhaps you are simply providing information.

As you answer the *What* question, you'll begin to form a mission, or a purpose for your presentation. We will talk more about developing your mission in the next chapter.

Why

Another important question you should answer is *Why* you are giving this presentation. Do you need to persuade, inform, or update the audience? Are you trying to inspire them to take action? Will you be presenting good news or bad? Answering these questions will help you further develop your mission.

Your presentation will be much different if your mission is to get the audience to do something—like approve the next budget or give you permission to take the next steps in a project—than it would be if you merely needed to inform or update them.

Who

It's important to know something about the audience you'll be addressing. *Who* are they, what do they now know, and do they have any preconceived notions about your topic? How many people are expected to attend?

Get as much information about your audience as possible, and well in advance of the presentation. If you know that you must present information to a negatively biased audience, you will undoubtedly prepare a little differently. You will pull together more facts, figures, and supporting documentation for this type of audience. Chances are you will also spend more time setting up your main topics. By contrast, if your audience includes experts or people already in agreement on the basics, then you can focus on your mission. You'll still need to introduce and position your main topics, but you can focus your presentation on new information. Tell them something they *don't* know.

When

Another basic question to answer is *When*. Obviously you'll need to know the exact day, date, and time. You'll also want to research these questions: Who are the other scheduled speakers? How much time do you have? Can the audience ask questions? Is this a mealtime event where you'll have to compete with clinking dishes and cups? Will you be speaking just after lunch, when some audience members might settle down for a nap if you dim the lights?

You should get a clear picture about how your presentation fits into the event schedule. If you are one of many speakers who will be addressing the audience, make sure you are comfortable with your position on the schedule. For example, if your role is to introduce a high-level overview of topics, you won't want to follow someone who just explained the most minute details of a sub-topic. How would the audience react after diving into details if you suddenly sent them into a stratospheric overview? Most meeting planners will prevent this from happening, but you can't always be sure that the people coordinating the meeting understand the nuances of the topics.

Where

Will you speak in a cramped conference room or in an exotic ballroom? What options will you have for audiovisual equipment? How about the room lighting—is it adjustable if you choose to bring in computer-driven visuals?

Answering the *Where* questions will help you mentally set the stage for delivering the presentation. It will also spare you the mistake of preparing the wrong kind of visual. For example, it may not be feasible to use overhead transparencies if the setting is a large room full of people. As the speaker you'll probably be perched up on a raised platform or stage, while the overhead projector is placed far away on the floor, out of reach. You'll be forced to enlist the help of an assistant to turn the pages of the presentation, creating an unnatural flow to the presentation.

Knowing where you'll be speaking allows you to choose the best audiovisual technique for the setting. In this case, a better alternative would be to use a computer with a wireless mouse or 35-mm slides with a remote control slide changer. I'll discuss high-tech solutions such as these in Chapter 6.

DEVELOPING AN ACTION PLAN

After you answer the five W's, you should have a sense of how much effort you'll need to put into the project. Proper planning for a presentation may take as many as 14 steps:

1. Developing the presentation plan; answering the five W's
2. Writing an outline; deciding what you are going to say
3. Researching the facts; adding third-party source content
4. Designing the visuals; choosing basics such as color or black and white, fonts, layout
5. Developing a storyboard; setting up your visuals
6. Producing samples; printing out visuals
7. Gaining approvals; testing with a pilot audience, the boss, or others
8. Piloting or rehearsing
9. Revising the storyboard, visuals, etc.
10. Producing final visuals
11. Creating handouts
12. Timing rehearsals; checking the timing and flow; preparing last-minute notes
13. Inspecting the presentation room; testing equipment, lights, etc.
14. Stepping through a final rehearsal complete with lights, equipment, and visuals

					January			

Sun	Mon	Tues	Wed	Thur	Fri	Sat
1	2 1st Production Meeting	3 Pres. Plan Presentation Design	4 Outline Research Samples	5 Presentation Design/Storyboard Approval	6	7
8	9	10 Revisions	11	12 Approval	13 Request A/V Eq	14 Print Handouts
15	16 Rehearsal	17 Check room	18 Room Setup Presentation Day	19	20	21
22	23	24	25	26	27	28

Figure 2-1   A sample presentation schedule

Scheduling Your Goals

Depending on the size of the event and the number of people you must coordinate with, you may want to use a project management software package and lay out the entire planning schedule with due dates. Since certain parts of the work will take more time than others, you'll find it helpful when you understand which tasks can overlap. Figure 2-1 shows how you can lay out the tasks on a project planner.

Whether you use a project management software package or simply tap entries into your electronic calendar, you should begin the planning process with due dates. It's a good idea to start with the date of the presentation and work backward.

Another important step in planning your presentation is to gather your resources, which include both people and tools. Unless your presentation is very short or based on work you've already developed, count on gathering a team of people to help you.

Choosing Your Tools

I suggest that you select a good presentation package early on. Most major software packages have taken the pain out of preparing outlines and visuals. They will save you time and frustration in preparing your notes and then converting your thoughts to attractive visuals.

You will also need to consider how you'll be delivering your presentation. Will you give a computer demo, or will you need to prepare 35-mm slides or overhead transparencies? Table 2-2 shows the type of tools you will need, your options, and my recommendations.

Table 2–2 Choosing the Best Tools for Your Mission

What You'll Need	Options Available	My Recommendations
Planning tools	• Word-processing software • An outliner • Pencil and paper	Tapping a few notes into a simple word-processing file usually gives you all the flexibility you'll need to answer basic planning questions. Make sure you answer the five W's as you create your initial plans.
Scheduling tools	• Electronic calendar • Project management software	If you are delivering a small presentation, then simply adding a few due dates on your electronic calendar will take care of most of your scheduling needs. Larger presentations involving teams of more than four members are best organized with project management software.
Development tools	• Word-processing software • An outliner • Presentation graphics software • Pencil and paper	For most occasions, you'll find that it is easiest to develop your project using a presentation graphics software package. Most popular packages let you create an outline, a storyboard, visuals, and speaker notes all in one place.

Table 2–2   Choosing the Best Tools for Your Mission (Continued)

What You'll Need	Options Available	My Recommendations
Delivery tools	• Personal computer • Wireless mouse • LCD panel overhead projector • Three-gun projector • Standard overhead projector • 35-mm slide projector	The personal computer-generated presentation is your best bet. Most software packages make it easy to add special effects and animation that will bring your presentation to life. I also suggest that you look into a wireless mouse, which gives you the most freedom to walk around the stage or presentation area. If you have a small or mid-sized room (one equipped for fewer than 100 people), you can easily use an LCD projection panel with a high-intensity overhead projector. If you use a larger room, consider a three-gun projector.
Handouts	• Black-and-white • Color • Notes from presentation software	Your handouts should be crisp and clean. For most audiences, black-and-white handouts prepared on a laser printer work fine. For special presentations, consider color handouts.

Today's personal computer market offers an abundance of good software to help you prepare a presentation. If you don't already have a favorite tool, I suggest that you look at the three top products in the category: PowerPoint by Microsoft, Freelance Graphics by Lotus Development Corporation, and Harvard Graphics for Windows by Software Publishing Corporation. All three packages run on a standard personal computer equipped with Microsoft Windows. See Chapter 6 for a more detailed discussion about these presentation tools.

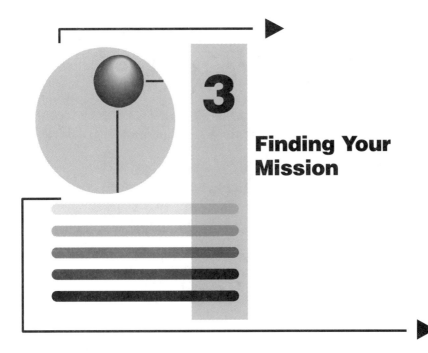

Finding Your Mission

The secret to making a good presentation is attention to detail. Planning for every situation and taking advantage of a few simple techniques will help you organize your presentation so it is easy to follow. And the easier you make it for your audience, the better your chances are to make your point.

Throughout this chapter, I build on the five W's that I introduced in Chapter 2. I'll teach you how to create an outline and flesh out the details. Also, you'll learn some helpful ways to start and end your presentation so that you gain the audience's interest in the beginning and then leave them thinking about your message.

To be successful, you need a plan—an *organized* plan. You should also keep a keen eye on making the presentation simple. If you can easily check off the points, the mission, and the message that you are trying to deliver, chances are that your audience will grasp the meaning of your presentation. And, of course, that's a big part of your objective: to make them understand what you have to say. The audience may not always agree with you and your assumptions, but they should at least understand what you are saying.

DEVELOPING THE "MISSION" MESSAGE: WHAT'S YOUR POINT?

Before you launch into the process of producing a presentation and visuals, you need to look at your answers to the five W's and ask a few more questions, like:

▶ What do you want to accomplish with the presentation?

▶ What's the point?

▶ What message are you trying to convey?

▶ Does the presentation need to fit a corporate style?

▶ Are you trying to inform, persuade, or do both?

▶ What does the audience need to see or hear before they'll believe in you?

▶ How will you present it to them?

Boil the message down to one sentence, put it on a yellow sticky note, and attach it to your computer monitor or desk. This way, you can look at it periodically and make sure you are still on track. Everything you say, do, or show during your presentation should support this message. Always keep it in mind.

For example, recently when I was asked to deliver a speech about developments in new information technology to an association of business brokers, I spent a lot of time figuring out what new innovations were pertinent to their world. Since these brokers often work for mid-sized, independent businesses, with a lot of salespeople calling on customers, I wanted to focus my technology selections on mobile computing, mapping software, global positioning systems, and e-mail. But the real focus of my talk wasn't individual technology, it was *"Better business through high technology."* That was the mission message. Since business people today can streamline many of their operations through the use of selected information technologies, I focused the entire speech around how these brokerages could use selected technology to improve their businesses.

Outlining Your Ideas

Almost every successful presentation starts with an outline. Many of us cringe when we think of putting together an outline, because we retain awful memories of hard-core schoolteachers who slapped our hands with a ruler if we mixed up major points and supporting points.

For business purposes, we needn't be so precise. A good presentation outline has just three levels:

- ▶ Topics
- ▶ Main points
- ▶ Sub-points

As you write the outline, pick three or four main topics you must discuss, making sure, of course, that they pertain to your objective. Group everything else around those few key subjects: your major points, then sub-points or supporting statements. Figure 3-1 shows five key topics of a presentation.

Deciding on Topics, Main Points, and Sub-points

Topics include the main ideas you are going to communicate. Most business presentations have two or three topics. In a longer speech or at a seminar, you might want to cover more ground, but you must be careful about presenting too many topics. An audience can only absorb so much. For example, in a presentation about the requirements for installing a new accounting system, you might list the following topics:

- ▶ Schedule
- ▶ Implementation plan
- ▶ Costs

These set up the main points of your presentation. Within the topics, you can then determine the main points.

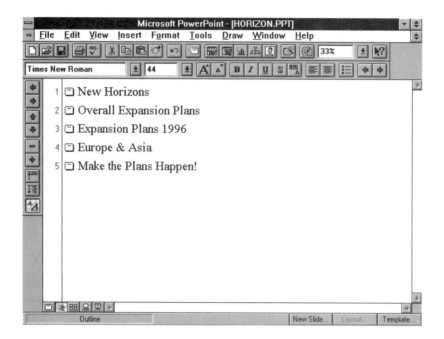

Figure 3–1 A simple outline can be the basis for a well-focused presentation.

The main points are what support your topics. A main point is one that you can make in a discussion or argument. For example, for the topic *Implementation Plan*, your main points might include:

▶ Initial system setup

▶ Technical review

▶ Employee training

▶ System cutover

▶ Quality review

Your sub-points should support the main points. Sub-points can provide rationale, defense, statistical proof, expert quotes or advice, or anything else that you find to uphold your main points. Remember to keep your sub-points quick and brief. It is more important to have quick, defensible proof than to over-explain every last detail. In most business situations, if your audience needs more details, they will ask for them. If your presentation doesn't allow time for many questions, you can prepare a detailed handout with supporting information.

Developing Your Main Points

Concentrate on your main points. Make sure each point supports the main objective. State the objective, placing the word *because* between it and the point you are stressing. Also, make sure you know the difference between features and benefits when you plan to make a call for action.

For example, this is a persuasive argument: "You should build your factory here" because "our town offers a skilled labor pool, low taxes and cost of living, and plenty of development land. Our town provides you everything you need to start a thriving business."

Your point: "You should build your factory here." The features you stress are a skilled labor pool, low taxes and cost of living, and plenty of development land available. The benefit to your audience is that your town provides everything they need to start a thriving business.

A main point should stand alone. For example, "You should build your factory here" is clearly a main point. The features, cost of labor, land, and so forth support the first point, so they should be used as sub-points, not as a main topic.

You can start thinking about your visuals once you've determined the main features of your talk. For the most part, your main topics will turn into text visuals (or text supplemented with a picture). Your sub-points become bullet points. See Figure 3-2 for an example of a detailed presentation outline. You can also consider using graphics to support your sub-points, especially if you have charted the numbers to prove these facts.

As a rule of thumb, main points should be supported by three sub-points. If you use fewer than three, make sure they are powerful ones. If you find yourself listing five or six sub-points, consider grouping them.

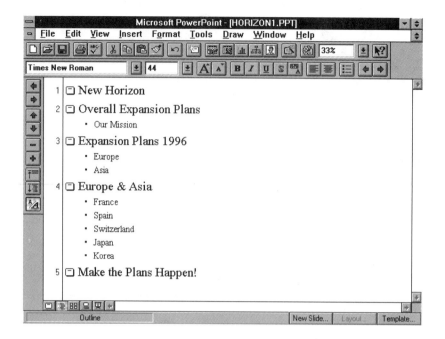

Figure 3-2   Presentation outline with points and sub-points

Common Presentation Strategies

Most good business presentations follow a three-step format: They have an opening, a middle (or a body), and a closing.

How you organize the flow of your speech depends on the type of presentation you are giving and what you hope to accomplish. Whichever method you choose, make sure you follow a logical order. Check your outline and make sure you can defend why you chose each topic, major point, and sub-point.

Here are some common examples:

Use the "problem/cause/solution" format when you want to elicit action from your audience. This format lets you set up (and win!) an argument, covering both problems and solutions within your speech:

1. Describe the problem.
2. Show why the current system isn't working (the cause of the problem).
3. Give information (pros and cons).
4. Suggest possible solutions.
5. Suggest an action you want the audience to follow.

The **"informative" format** works best when you need to provide a status update. This format is excellent when your mission is to present the status of a project or an update on research:

1. Give an overview.
2. Go through each point, giving details as you go along.
3. Present your findings.
4. Summarize the findings.

The **"chronological" format** presents information by date. It works best when you must give your audience a perspective of how a series of events took place over time:

1. Give an overview.
2. Present major events or milestones, starting with the oldest one and moving to the most current.
3. Present the current status.
4. Summarize findings and call for action if necessary.

You can use a "compare and contrast" format for presentations that show information with great similarities or differences. For example, if you need to explain the differences between TV sales in the U.S. versus Japan, this format would be appropriate:

1. Give an overview.
2. Present major topics; show the results or data for one group and then the other.
3. Summarize your findings.

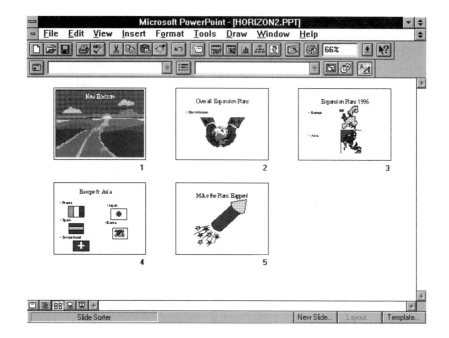

Figure 3-3   Shape of your presentation: a short opening, a well supported body, and a quick close

---

Remember—"Tell them what you are going to tell them; then tell them; then tell them what you told them." It's a good idea to work on the middle or body of your presentation before you struggle with finding the perfect introduction or closing. See the sample presentation shape in Figure 3-3.

Tools You'll Need

To get started, you can use either an outline on your favorite word-processing software or a presentation graphics software package. Both provide excellent tools for entering and manipulating, organizing and reorganizing ideas.

Since many people are comfortable with basic word-processing software such as WordPerfect or Microsoft Word, they find it easier to build the outline using those familiar tools, entering and organizing the basic topics, main points, and sub-points there. When they are finished fleshing out the basic outline, they convert the data to a presentation package, such as Harvard Graphics, PowerPoint, or Freelance Graphics.

Some very experienced presenters bypass the word processor and enter all their initial and revised thoughts directly into the outline facility of their presentation software. Since the major packages all support editing and spell-checking functions, these presenters save time by using the same software from concept to completion.

Which method you choose is a matter of personal style. I recommend that you try both approaches and figure out what makes you most comfortable. What's important is that you document information and keep a list of all the little details that support your outline as you create it. You will want to refer to those details when you start developing the actual presentation.

Fact or Opinion?

The two general types of information are facts and opinions. When you gather facts, make sure you document the sources. You probably won't include all the details of your sources in your presentation speech or on your visuals, but you can use your sources in your supporting materials, such as a handout, or have them on hand in case someone questions you or wants to do independent research. The minimum information you need is the author's name, the source (magazine name and article title, book title, report title), and date published.

If you get information from other people, make sure they are "respected" sources. Think about the source of the information: Are they biased because of their surroundings? For example, if your topic was water pollution, would you get information from the EPA, a chemical plant, or an environmental activist group? Perhaps all three! But if you cite only the information you get from the chemical plant, your audience might not feel that information is credible.

Make sure your audience will respect your source. If you are speaking to a group of medical specialists about weight control, chances are that your audience would believe the information you cite from the *Journal of American Medicine* more than they would the latest diet fad covered in the *National Enquirer.* I talk more about pulling together research information in the next chapter.

When you state your own opinions, you don't have to provide as many details as you do for facts. You should, however, be prepared to explain how you developed your opinion on each topic or main point.

For example, if you don't believe that a project can be successful because it is underfunded, you might want to prepare a short list of other projects that were underfunded and failed, or cite all the needs of the project in question and add up their costs. Either way, you will give your audience some rational and defensible reasons for your opinion.

Consider a Script

Many professional presenters wouldn't think of writing a script. In fact, most courses and books strongly advise people to forgo trying to script every last word.

I take exception to the common advice. I think that by scripting *parts* of a presentation, you can work through the wording more easily. If you don't often speak in front of a group, chances are that giving the presentation will prove stressful. And under stress people can get tongue-tied and forget everything, including their own colleagues' names. I know one presenter who got so flustered when he started a comparison of two products that he ended up confusing the product attributes. He also confused the audience to the point that they simply tuned out his message (and him).

Scripting certain elements of your presentation can help you get the story straight. It can help you put your words together so they flow well and don't sound stilted.

I recommend that, if you do try to script some words, you create paragraphs of text explaining your topics, main points, or sub-points. You don't need pages full of text, just a few well thought-out phrases.

CHOOSING THE RIGHT TONE

Choose a tone before writing your script or notes. Will your talk be polished and professional, or relaxed? Action-packed? Depending on your message and the audience, you may want to stick to exact, correct grammar or use more casual language.

In most cases you should avoid jargon, *unless* it is the common vocabulary of your audience. For example, a highly technical audience expects the speaker to use the lingo of the profession. Where possible, however, provide a little help and define acronyms.

For example, the speaker at a conference of bank loan officials talked about mortgage options. During the question-and-answer period that followed, someone from the audience asked, "What future do you see for A.R.M.'s?" The speaker, unsure if everyone in the audience knew what an A.R.M. was, answered, "The market for adjustable rate mortgages is solid today but might change over the next two years because of fluxes in basic interest rates."

The speaker gave the questioner a direct answer and also helped those who weren't quite sure of what the question was about.

If you do use industry jargon or acronyms, make sure you pronounce them correctly. You will instantly lose credibility with most of the audience if you don't know the lingo. This happened to one speaker when he talked to a technical audience about software and incorrectly pronounced a product name as "sap," when industry professionals knew it by the initials S.A.P. A good general rule: If you're not sure, don't say it.

Holding Audience Interest

Obviously your presentation will be more effective if you keep the audience's attention. Ask yourself, Would I sit through this presentation? Consider some techniques for forming your words:

▶ **Use short, effective words familiar to the audience.** Long words delay your message, while short words are effective, fast, and direct. For example, use words like *check, confirm,* or *proof* instead of *verification.*

▶ **Use simple sentences—noun and verb.** Don't interrupt the flow by over-explaining, adding too many ideas or modifiers, or too much jargon. When you speak, keep your sentences short so people can get "sound bites" filled with information or a succinct message.

▶ **Use the active voice.** Active-voice speech keeps the audience involved. Make the subject of your sentences perform the action. For example look at the difference between the following two sentences:

- *Active:* The supervisor records all details.
- *Passive:* The details are recorded by the supervisor.

▶ **Use action verbs.** You can increase the pacing of your presentation through powerful verbs. Where possible, avoid forms of the verb "to be," such as *am, is, are, was,* and *were.*

- *Weak:* The seat *was* designed for comfort.
- *Stronger:* We designed the seat for comfort.

▶ **Be logical and concise.** Make your point and keep it simple. Support your topic in a logical order. Don't confuse the audience.

Honoring Short Attention Spans

We live in a fast-paced society—these days we see things moving by at breakneck speeds. We demand fast food, fast cars, and quick deals. Few people want to sit through anything—including a business presentation—that drags on and on.

In order to keep up, you must be concise. Don't waste time explaining things people already know; only explain new ideas or concepts. Boil your points down to bullet items whenever possible. Make sure your information is to the point.

For example, if you use a research study to defend one of your points, simply cite the most compelling part of the research. Don't waste people's time (or risk them tuning out) by giving every last detail of the research, telling how it was conducted, and naming all 27 people who participated in the project.

Ask yourself how long *you* pay attention to what someone is saying before your mind starts to wander. Probably not for very long. Keep in mind that even when someone has time to listen to you, he or she can only absorb so much information at one time. Many people's attention spans are only about 30 seconds long.

People today are used to getting "sound bites"—they receive information like this all the time on TV and the radio. Structure your thoughts and information this way—especially if you are covering information they should already know. "Sound bites" are also a good way to illustrate a point you've already made.

Finally, plan for a pause every now and then, especially in long presentations. In between each topic or major point, give your audience a little breathing time before you move on to the next important point.

Above all, remember: Keep it short. Keep it brief. Keep it visual. Your audience will appreciate it.

GREAT OPENINGS AND CLOSINGS

Business presenters often complain that the hardest part of a presentation is developing the beginning and the end. Yet these are often the most important elements of your speech—the parts people are likely to remember.

The introduction takes up a small portion of your speech, but it must accomplish a great deal. It should capture the audience's attention and imagination. It sets the stage for your presentation, telling the group what you are going to cover, what your goals are, and what you want of them.

Likewise, developing a powerful closing is critical. The closing gives you a chance to reinforce key messages and make a call for action. If you don't tell your audience what you want them to do next, you miss a great opportunity to make something happen.

Open with a Bang!

There is no single, sure-fire, "works every time" way to open a speech. It's a matter of personal style. Most experienced presenters vary the openings of speeches by picking the most appropriate technique for the topic and the one they can deliver most effectively.

Ways to start a presentation include anecdotes, analogies, quotes, strong opinions, or references to the occasion (the weather, the attendees, and so on). Whatever you choose, it should grab your audience's attention and be relevant to your message. If you are at a loss about where to begin, continue on for my suggestions.

Create Common Ground

A good way to open a speech is to put yourself on the same level as the audience. You can bond quickly if you show them you are human and walk (or have walked) in their shoes. If you can refer to something that they face every day, or a present situation, you'll make them feel comfortable right away.

For example, to welcome a group of new employees into the company, one manager began his presentation with a few words about his first day at the company and talked a bit about his early experiences there: how uneasy he felt trying to find the company cafeteria, how he was embarrassed to ask directions to the restroom, and how he lost his car in the mammoth employee parking lot. His presentation successfully disarmed the new employees and made them feel more comfortable.

Tell Them What You're *Not* Going to Say

Sometimes you need to let the audience know, up front, what you are and are not going to talk about. It helps set the stage and gives you control over the agenda, the topics, and later the types of questions your audience will ask.

People in public life often begin by stating what issue they plan to speak about and which topics are off-limits. For example, look at a presidential news conference. The chief politician will often say something like, "Good morning, ladies and gentlemen. We're here to talk about health care reform and not the erroneous rumors reported on last night's news about new taxes."

That kind of direct opening, albeit a bit terse, accomplishes two things. First, it sets the stage and ground rules for the topic at hand: health care. Second, the President puts the report of new taxes off-limits by saying it was false and that it wouldn't be discussed at the news conference.

Start with a Good Quote

Famous quotes provide an effective way to open a presentation, *if* the quote fits. Quotes can set the stage and mindset and often foretell what is about to come.

Quotes, as introductions, should be short and well rehearsed. To be effective, they usually require the speaker to recite the quote with a little dramatic flair.

If you can find a quote that sums up your message, don't be afraid to use it. If you need help finding a suitable quote, check out some of the low-cost software that indexes quotes by author, topic, and key words.

Read from the Dictionary

If you can't find exactly the right famous quote, but want to start out with authority, try quoting the dictionary. You can make a positive opening statement if you find a concise dictionary definition of a special word relevant to your presentation.

Dictionary definitions of verbs are especially effective. Consider a presentation where you are trying to get the audience to change something. You might start with defining a word like *progress* or *change.*

In other cases, you might want to define a new concept, like *empowerment, knowledge-based work,* or *team management.*

Defining words can help your audience focus on your topic and absorb your message faster and easier.

Give Them a Jolt

Some speakers make effective use of a statement that surprises the audience. I once heard a technology evangelist, known for sending as many as 7,000 e-mail messages a day, start his presentation by telling the audience that he didn't think e-mail would ever fly. Surely his audience didn't expect that statement coming from him, and they listened intently for how he would follow up this seemingly out-of-character comment.

Using the unexpected jolt doesn't work well for all speakers. You must be able to effectively use a little drama and know how to pause so that your audience can take in what you have just said. If you are in doubt about whether you can pull off this technique, try out your opening in front of an honest friend or a video camera.

Take It from the Headlines

The morning paper sometimes provides an excellent opening for a presentation. If you are trying to prove the importance and timeliness of your topic, there's no better hook than to relate it to something currently in the news.

If you use the headlines to open your speech, it helps to bring the actual paper or magazine as a prop. You might even underline and read a short (15- to 20-word) passage directly from the article. This technique can provide a wake-up call to the audience, telling them that they better listen to your message to stay on top of things.

"On This Day in History…"

You can develop an effective opener by giving your audience a sense of history or position. This technique works well when your underlying message is *"My, how different things are,"* or *"The more things change, the more they stay the same."*

For example, I once opened a speech by sharing with the audience that it was the 21st anniversary of the bar-code. "Just think about it," I said, "how on earth did we ever buy our groceries in the old days?" I spent a few minutes reminding them of the cumbersome process that grocery store clerks had to endure, then related it to modern times. The opener worked well, since the audience was about to embark on implementing a new technology that would render many of their old business processes obsolete.

Get Personal

A good way to humanize a presentation is to open with a personal story that relates to your main topics. Real-life stories about your kids can be an excellent source of material that provide a humorous, innocent, and sometimes heartwarming picture.

Personal experiences help establish rapport with the audience and often make them smile and prepare to listen to you.

When talking about the future of computing in society, I often open my speeches with a short story about my electronically empowered daughter. She started sending me e-mail messages at the age of nine. She turned this activity into "electronic mom manipulation" by age 11 when she started sending me her Christmas shopping list by e-mail.

Lots of people in the audience can relate to the activities and antics of precocious children.

Find a Hook

How do you grab your audience's attention? Create your own hook. Hooks are like headlines. We read them in newspapers, look at them on billboards, hear them on the radio, and watch them on TV. They are what makes us want more information, so that we pay attention to what is said next.

To keep the audience excited, entranced, bewitched, and interested, you might try this technique. Create your hook by answering the following questions:

- ▶ What's the most interesting part of your presentation?
- ▶ What's the most humorous part of your presentation?
- ▶ What's the most unusual part of your presentation?
- ▶ Can you capture this information in one sentence?

The hook must relate or lead to your objective. It must excite or interest your audience. It should fit with your audience and the style of your presentation.

Hooks work great as an opener—just decide if you want to ask a question or make a statement. If you make it a question, you must present an answer in your speech. Your hook can also relate to current affairs, so there's immediate affinity with the audience. The hook can be dramatic or humorous, but make sure it's positive.

Tell a Joke

Provided that it is appropriate to the situation, using humor establishes a rapport with your audience. It helps break the ice and sets people at ease. It makes your audience like you.

Humor can also reinforce your point. For example, a senator was making a speech on the high cost of medical care. He joked, "I went to the doctor yesterday with a sore throat. He told me to come back when I had something more expensive." The senator made his point, and the audience was amused.

Humor can also be used to break the ice with the audience. Use humor between points to give the audience time to relax. One-liners, if you decide to use them, should flow smoothly and naturally into your speech. But don't try to be a comedian.

Where can you find humorous anecdotes? The best place (and a safe source) is *Reader's Digest.* You can also find jokes and cartoons in the newspaper. The late-night talk shows and the small children in your life come up with some great one-liners. If you hear something funny, write it down.

Avoid ethnic and off-color jokes, period. Before telling a joke, ask someone else what they think. Examine it for ethnic, racist, sacrilegious, sexist, or other offensive content. If you're not certain, don't use it. The best jokes are those that identify with the situation the audience is in.

What if no one laughs? What if someone sneezes just as you are giving the punch line? What's funny is extremely subjective—it depends on you (your timing) and your audience (their mood). If a joke bombs, just move on. Pretend it never happened and get on with your presentation. (You probably won't want to use the same joke again, though.)

Effective Closings

The conclusion is your final chance to drive your point home. It should cover all of your final goals:

➤ Restate the main points.

➤ Offer recommendations and solutions.

➤ Ask for action from the audience.

Avoid limp endings like "In conclusion," or "I see our time is up." End with a bang, make a point. A quote or a dramatic statement can be a great way to close out your speech.

Recently I ended a speech with a sense of fear. The topic was how companies could (and some actually did) use information technology to radically reinvent themselves. These were my closing comments:

> *Just picture it…the people working in the consummate company of the 21st century. They are active, agile, and aware. They know how to harness the best of teams, techniques, and technologies. They share a vision, and boy can they execute. Pretty neat, huh? Now…picture competing with this company.*

I could hear gasps from the audience. They got my message; my closing comments merely sealed it.

For presentation closings, you can use many of the same techniques as you would for openings. You can tie the end to your opening, or use a new technique. It is a matter of preference.

Predict the Future

One effective way to close is to share a glimpse of the future. You don't need to pull out a crystal ball (although it might provide a cute prop), but you can take your audience out into tomorrow and tomorrow's tomorrow. Show how the quality of life will change if the recommendations you have made in your speech are carried out.

Appeal to Their Emotions

A good technique for closing is to appeal to your audience's emotions—either personal or professional. For example, if the company mission is to be the best, cheapest, fastest delivery organization in its class, then appeal to those goals. If the company managers want to be the brightest, then appeal to that goal.

Don't be afraid to use fear or greed in your appeal. Interestingly, many people in business are motivated by this drive more than any other.

Create a Call for Action

Ask yourself, What do I want from my listeners?—and then ask for it. You usually want the audience to act upon the information you have presented, or you want them to react a certain way. Make sure you specifically state what you want.

You might even offer specific suggestions for action, for example: "Please write down three ideas about doing this project and get back to me by next Tuesday." Here you are asking for a specific action by a definite time.

In a sense, you are "asking for the order." You may not think you are selling anything, but you are. You are selling your ideas and concepts.

Ask for Questions

Many audiences appreciate a chance to ask questions. They might not have understood one or more of your points, they might want to add reinforcing anecdotes, or they may wish to share some comments or concerns.

Sometimes it takes a little priming to get people to start talking. If no one breaks the ice with a first question, ask *yourself* a question. You can say "People often ask me   " Then answer the question you've posed.

As a general rule of thumb, you should keep the question-and-answer period short. Most speeches are scheduled in half-hour increments. Table 3-1 helps you figure out the timing for your speech and the question-and-answer period.

Table 3–1   Alloting Time for Questions and Answers

Total Presentation Time	Time Spent Delivering Your Message	Question & Answer Period
30 min.	20-25 min.	5-10 min.
45 min.	30-40 min.	5-15 min.
60 min.	45 min.	15 min.
90 min.	60-75 min.	15-30 min.

VISUALIZING SUCCESS

It's never too soon to start practicing. As soon as you flesh out your outline and construct your opening and closing, then you should try it out.

Picture yourself being introduced, walking to the front of the room, adjusting the microphone and your speaker notes, and beginning to talk.

Many successful business presenters rehearse their presentations in pieces. They might talk through the opening as they drive to work in the morning, or think through the main topics as they watch the nightly news.

If the presentation is very important to your career, get out (or rent) a video recorder. Prop it up and take a video of your practice session. Pretend that the lens of the camera is your audience and try to make eye contact with it. You don't have to record the entire presentation from start to finish, but make sure you record enough to capture your facial expressions, hand movements, and gestures. If you need to work on them, now is a good time to start. You might even want to skip forward to Chapter 8, where I discuss speaking techniques.

The more you do now, the easier it will be to deliver your presentation. To paraphrase an old saying, the best business presentations are not written, but *re*written…and re-said, and rehearsed.

In the next chapter, I'll work on refining the message.

Fine-tuning the Message with Research

If you completed the steps presented in Chapter 3, you are well on your way to developing an effective presentation. By now you have a mission, an outline, a structure, an opening, and a closing. Are you almost done? No.

In a sense, you've just begun. You have the blueprint and framework, but you still have much more work ahead if you really want to deliver a polished presentation. You have your mission and your message, but do you have enough facts to support it? Will you be convincing enough if you just present your own opinions?

Chances are that you will fail to convince anyone of anything unless you bring along some supporting evidence. Even experts cite other experts when they want to prove a point.

This chapter focuses on fine-tuning the message for your presentation with research—namely computer-assisted research. It discusses techniques and places to look for honing in on the message and gathering more facts. Most importantly, it introduces new ways to check your facts and expand your reach. If you have never used a personal computer and modem as a research assistant, you are in for a treat. There really is a world of information available. The communications-equipped computer will be one of the most powerful research tools you've ever had.

FOCUSING YOUR RESEARCH

The key to researching a business presentation is knowing what questions to ask and how to ask them. Experienced presenters rely on their own knowledge of the topic and then augment their knowledge by citing academic research and business or technological publications. A little history sprinkled in here and there can also help.

As you review your outline, jot down some questions that you think your audience might ask—or look for weak spots in your outline that need shoring up with some facts or research. It helps to organize your questions before you start researching. Consider making a table of questions and good places to look. Table 4-1 shows an example.

Creative Number-Crunching

Where possible, include meaningful statistics in your presentation. It helps if you know the basics, like *who* and *how many.* If you have access to market research information, all the better.

Try to create a list of questions and focus on the questions that have numerical answers. Feel free to turn the numbers into percentages or to compare them to some other set of figures.

Years ago, former president Ronald Reagan made a convincing speech by illustrating a huge number with a visual metaphor. Referring to the budget deficit, he remarked that if those dollars were laid end to end, they would reach the moon. If you use a creative technique like this, make sure your calculations are reasonably correct, since it would be a shame to lose credibility by expressing your data inaccurately.

If you can't answer a specific question with a specific fact, try asking and answering another question. You may not ever resolve all

Table 4–1 Sample Questions and Sources for Answers

Question	Possible Source	Where to Look
How many multimedia-equipped personal computers have been purchased?	• Research service • Government survey • Other surveys • Trade magazine article • Business magazine article	• Dialog • Internet • All on-line services • Business magazine database • Dow-Jones News Service
What are the market prospects for multimedia personal computers in the future?	• Research service • Government survey • Other surveys • Trade magazine article • Business magazine article	• Dialog • Internet • All on-line services • Business magazine database or CD-ROM • Dow-Jones News Service • CD-ROMs

the fact-finding needs of your presentation, but if you employ the right tools, you undoubtedly will gather enough to making a convincing and informative presentation.

THE DARK AGES OF RESEARCH

As a business presenter, you have plenty of options when looking for research. You can search through stacks of trade publications in the corporate library, research files or reports maintained by your department colleagues, visit the local library, read the thick computer reports produced by your information services department, and on and on. No doubt you can spend a lot of time going from place to place.

For some corporate business presenters, the steps involved with research haven't changed in 20 years. It still involves lots of effort and drudgery.

Sometimes you can't get an answer to a specific question. According to the American Library Association, your chances of getting a question answered completely and correctly in a standard library search are about 50-50. That goes for academic libraries as well as public libraries. Don't count on easily finding a bibliographical reference item, either. If you go to a library looking for an exact cited reference, your chances of walking out with it are less than 40 percent.

In fact, it reminds me a little of my senior year in college. Let me share the opening of one of my recent speeches about the effort I put into researching material for a report:

> *As a college senior, I undertook a project to write an extensive research paper. Mind you, this wasn't just any research paper. It was the research paper, the best, the most comprehensive, the most wonderful research paper any college senior would ever write.*
>
> *With that goal in mind, I trucked off to the Library of Congress in Washington, D.C. Day after countless day I would show up early in the morning, grab a parking space, and run to the front of the library, where I would begin going through the catalogs, looking for the books that I needed for that day's research. I would dutifully fill out the book request forms and then turn them in to one of the clerks. The clerk would then assign my book requests to a runner who would go after the books from the Library of Catacombs. The wait was so long I sometimes felt the runner went to Baltimore and back to get my books. When the books were given to me, I would seek out the most quiet corner of the library, sit down, read as fast as I could, and take as many notes as I could possibly scratch out on a piece of paper. At the end of the day I would have to turn in all of my books, because at the Library of Congress you're not allowed to check the books out and take them home. I'd run back to the car, go back to my apartment, transcribe my notes from hieroglyphics into English, think of what I needed for the next day's research, and then go back and start the process all over again the following day.*
>
> *The good news about my research methodology was that I learned a lot about the subject and I did receive a very good grade for my efforts. The bad news was that it took forever. As I recall, it*

took about six months to get the research project done. When I look at what I went through, only about an hour to two hours of every day was spent actually reading and learning the materials. The rest of the time was spent waiting for the research materials to come to me at the Library of Congress, or writing down my notes, or transcribing my notes from my shorthand into English so I could remember what I had read. In all, my notes would be transcribed three times: from the book to shorthand to longhand and finally into a summarized version that made it into the research paper I was writing.

What's interesting to note about this story is that today I could bring up virtually all of the research on my computer screen in a matter of minutes or hours. With a computer, modem, and a little know-how about accessing the Internet or commercial on-line services, I could quickly find nearly every fact that I once spent six months tracking down.

THE COMPUTER: YOUR NEW RESEARCH ASSISTANT!

It takes a little know-how in order to use the computer as a research tool. Today, you can access volumes of research information from the comfort of your home or office. Most people use computer research tools from one or two different media—using a CD-ROM drive and a few of the CD-ROM–based libraries or dialing into on-line services with a modem.

If you are new to computer-assisted research, make sure you build a little extra time into your schedule. You will need the time to get familiar with *where and how* to find information. While some on-line services can ferret out and serve up facts in a matter of seconds or minutes, finding the right places to look will take hours for the uninitiated. You should learn a few of the search techniques and a little bit about constructing search questions (covered later in this chapter).

Moreover, don't expect to become an instant expert researcher. Computer-assisted research tools are still relatively new, and the path to the right information is still largely uncharted. You can visualize the experience of working with them as walking into a vast research library but having no card catalog or indexing system to find anything. Intimidating, yes, but not impossible.

The CD-ROM Connection

There is a plethora of products available that capture and store information on relatively inexpensive CD-ROM discs. New titles appear almost daily, and already a dizzying array of discs offer everything from the entire United States phone directory to a talking, video-enhanced version of *The Guinness Book of World Records.* Pemberton Press, publishers of *CD-ROM Professional,* estimated that there were over 6,000 CD-ROM titles in circulation by 1994. About half of them contain full-text documents rather than just abstracts.

A number of trade and business magazines are also available as CD-ROM subscriptions. It is possible today to get several years' worth of periodical information from companies such as BusinessWeek, Ziff Publishing Company, CMP, or IDG Publishers. Generally these services cost between $300 and $900 a year, and the supplier mails the updated CD-ROM to the customer about once a month or quarterly, depending on the service. Other CD-ROM–based information subscriptions are also available to those with special interests, such as law or medicine. These services are generally more expensive, sometimes from $2,000 to $20,000 per year. Despite what appears to be a high-cost product, they do save companies money when used by a number of people in an organization.

CD-ROM–based solutions provide an ideal solution for people needing very focused sets of information. They are less suitable for more general research requiring multiple sources. For example, since many CD-ROM subscription packages offer just one publisher's version of the facts, a business presenter in need of more variety could waste lots of time flipping different discs in and out of a CD player all day.

Commercial On-line Services

A more flexible solution than CD-ROMs, albeit sometimes a more costly one, is to obtain subscriptions to various business and professional news services. For example, both CompuServe and the Dow Jones News Service are excellent sources, offering access to multiple trade and industry periodicals as well as news wires coming from the Dow Jones Wire Service, Reuters, UPI, AP, and various other news sources. General Electric's Information Service, GEnie, also provides access to excellent business research with its gateways to third-party services.

The collection of information and the on-line research available is nothing short of phenomenal. These services bring together information from many different environments and give true meaning to the phrase *information at your fingertips*.

Subscribing to a Clipping Service

Some on-line services, such as CompuServe and the Dow Jones News Service, allow subscribers to put together electronic clipping folders that clip articles on selected topics only from certain selected periodicals. And these topics can be specified in a single word, such as *reengineering,* or the research can even be narrowed down to exact niches like *reengineering in a manufacturing environment.*

As information, stories, or news wires are published on the selected topics, they are automatically clipped and placed in the customer's file folder. Some services even allow for news alerts! You can set up the clippings folders to automatically forward a news story to your electronic mailbox.

To Push or Be Pulled?

Electronic clipping services started the notion of the "push" information model. These services go out and work on behalf of the reader—prescreening stories and collecting only those of interest. In a sense, they "push" information out to you.

The other information model, the "pull" model, looks a lot more like classic research. You go to the information source and pull out the information that you need. You must look for information; it won't find you.

You'll probably spend much of your time working with tools that let you "pull" information. If you regularly make presentations about a particular topic, or if you need to constantly stay updated, you should look for services that "push" information to you. That way, you'll find it easier to stay on top of the latest breaking news.

Your Own Robot

Business presenters and other knowledge professionals need to capitalize on intelligent agents, or software robots that search out information and perform tasks on your behalf. According to *Online Magazine,* in 10 years we will be hooked up to more than a trillion objects of useful knowledge. No single person or direct manipulation interface could ever handle that. People won't sit down with a super search and start fishing around the entire world for things that might be of use to them. Instead, the intelligent computer agents will work tirelessly as round-the-clock retrievers that are constantly firing away, searching for things.

In many ways, electronic clipping services from commercial on-line services resemble primitive forms of electronic agents or robots. But clipping and holding information is only the beginning.

Agent technology is very powerful, because it provides automatic access and automatic work on behalf of the user. A new form of this technology was announced early in 1994 by a company called General Magic. Their product, Telescript, promises to provide extraordinarily well tuned and highly functioning agent capability.

Telescript, as it evolves, will not only go out and seek and pull information for the user, but it will actually help you make decisions. Potentially, technology like Telescript could make your plane reservations and put you in the proper seat. It could go get your theater tickets for you, or it could create your shopping list.

Agent technology is available from some services today. For example, First! by Individual Incorporated goes one step further by using sophisticated filtering techniques. In addition to culling information from many different sources, both news and industry periodicals, the service uses artificial intelligence techniques that go far beyond what is capable with a simple search for keywords. The First! service offers specially trained research assistants who help you configure your searches. Then, once the search is set up, the software agents take over and look for appropriate placement of search terms within articles, and filter appropriate news media. Like other services, when an article or news story matches your search criteria, the service will send the electronically clipped information to you.

In early 1994, a low-cost pioneer entered the market with sophisticated agent technology. Farcast introduced information "Droids"— information robots that help find and filter information for the reader. For subscription prices of less than $1 a day, Farcast offers engaging content, powerful features, and a straightforward interface. It covers a collection of news sources, industry-wide press releases, and stock quotes. The most powerful part of Farcast's service does "push" information to the reader, but the company also offers a "pull" option. You can ask its Droid to search new articles that are up to 30 days old.

Other On-Line Services

Another service that provides similar search and retrieval capabilities is Lexis, by Mead Data Systems. This service primarily focuses on the legal profession.

Dialog, which combines many different database services, is among the most powerful of the on-line services. Dialog also cooperates with other services, such as GEnie and CompuServe, by serving as the warehouse for some of the databases.

In fact, there are so many informational databases that there is a directory of databases. The Gale Directory of Databases, from Gale Research, Inc., provides a comprehensive guide to publicly available databases worldwide. It covers databases of all types in all subject areas. The Gale Directory contains descriptions of 5,300 databases that are accessible through more than 820 on-line services, plus more than 3,500 databases available on CD-ROM, diskette, or magnetic tape.

You might even find information to support your presentation on some of the on-line services geared toward home users. Services such as Delphi, America Online, and Prodigy lack some of the more sophisticated search tools, and they don't offer in-depth retrieval for industry news. They do, however, offer searching of business and news magazines. For example, America Online posts *Time* magazine and other news sources.

The Internet

Finally, no discussion of searching for information with a computer would be complete without mentioning the Internet—the worldwide network of connected computers. The Internet connects millions of people through a web of thousands of host computers. Originally established by the U.S. government in 1969 as a place for government researchers to store information, the Internet is truly the granddaddy of on-line services. Use of the Internet is free, but you must pay an Internet access provider to establish an Internet connection to your computer. Once on the Internet, you have myriad information sources at your disposal. Many universities from around the globe participate, making available research on all kinds of topics. The bad news is that it can be quite a challenge to find them all.

Innovations such as the World Wide Web and Mosaic and searching tools with fun names like Archie and Veronica make finding your areas of interest somewhat easier, but unfortunately the complexities of the Internet are beyond the scope of this book. If you decide to get connected, you'll find many good books all about the Internet at your local bookstore.

If you are already an Internet user, chances are you have some favorite places to look up information. If you are not an experienced user, save your foray onto the Internet until you have time to learn the basics and the nuances.

Limiting Search Criteria

Wherever you do research, you want to make sure you are asking the right questions. That's a given. But when you use computer-assisted research tools, you also want to make sure you ask the questions right—that is, in the right format.

Table 4–2 Search Qualifiers

Search Term	How It Works	Example of a Search
and	Lets you narrow your search to all documents that contain both words.	leather and shoes
or	Widens the search to include documents that contain either word.	leather or shoes
not	Focuses search on those documents with one word but not the other.	shoes not vinyl
near or n#	Includes only documents with both words, within # words of each other.	leather n10 shoes
?	Includes documents that have any letter following the entry. For example, *shoe make?* selects *shoe maker*, but not *shoe making*.	shoe make?
*	Includes documents with any word that begins with the entry. For example, *shoe mak** selects articles with the words *shoe maker*, *shoe makers*, and *shoe making*.	shoe mak*

Although every search service can have its own language, most follow similar conventions for phrasing search questions. Many systems allow you to specify or exclude words, create phrases, and narrow searches to certain time periods. For example, if you needed to search for information on recent imports of leather shoes into the United States, you would most likely ask some of the questions shown in Table 4-2.

Most systems also let you specify dates with terms like *before, after,* and *between.* You would construct search limits like these:

▶ Before 1/31/95
▶ After 10/28/93
▶ Between 1/1/90 and 2/4/95

These phrases quickly limit the number of documents that you'll have to wade through. Information tends to have a shelf life. Whether you are talking about management practices or high technology, timeliness is often important.

For most business research, you need to search only the most recent articles, those published within the last two years. In some cases, you may wish to go back further. Most business searchers avoid going back more than five years.

The five-year rule holds true with old-fashioned library searches as well. According to a report by the American Library Association, a book that has sat on the shelves for years in an academic setting rarely circulates. People simply don't use yesterday's news very often.

The Information Highway: Pitfalls and Potholes

If reading this chapter has made you want to speed around your office until you can get a hook-up to the information superhighway—wait! Plan your trip wisely and get to know where the best sources of research are for your particular topic. Also, be wary of getting distracted. On-line searches can pull up all sorts of interesting but irrelevant information. You will avoid wasting time if you stay focused on your research path and don't stray off-course by looking up tangential items.

In Part II, I turn your attention to the details of design and style. The next few chapters will help you take the information you have gathered and use the computer to put the data in presentation form so you can share it with others.

PRODUCING

By now the *content* of your presentation should be taking shape. You should have a clear idea of what you are going to say, how you are going to say it, and how you can defend your position. In your mind, you stand ready to deliver.

You need to turn your attention now to the details of *design* and *style.* With an eye toward style, you have an opportunity to take what's in your head and use the computer to help you put the information in such a way that others can understand it.

No longer the domain of skilled professionals with creative natures and graphics-arts training, creating stunning presentations is within the reach of most businesspeople. The only catch: know-how. Even if you can't draw a straight line, don't know one end of the color wheel from another, or can't remember the difference between a serif and sans serif font, you can still make dazzling visuals—thanks to the personal computer and low-cost software, printers, and projection devices.

Part II starts by introducing the background elements of layout, type, and color. Then I cover the special features of popular presentation software. Your personal choice for software depends on your individual tastes and sometimes your corporate or industry selection. Finally I make a case for multimedia presentation packages that let you not only add color and clever graphics, but sound and animation. These capabilities add richness and power to your presentation.

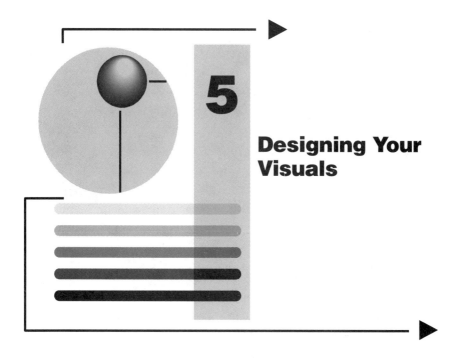

5

Designing Your Visuals

Visual aids can make a big difference in your presentation—a positive or negative one. Effective visuals draw your audience into your presentation and provide stimulation that keeps them interested (or at least awake). Good visuals explain, enhance, and reinforce the information you are trying to convey, increasing the audience's retention.

The right visuals can enhance your professional image and influence your audience's attitude about your message. In addition, they can serve as cues in your speech, guiding you through your points and observations so you won't have to read from a prepared script. Moreover, visuals help you keep on track and allow you to return to your points smoothly after an interruption or digression.

Bad visuals, on the other hand, mar your professional image. Not only can they bore the audience, but they may evoke the wrong type of response. They can overshadow the rest of your presentation, entertaining without educating. Your visuals should support you and your message and help the audience create a picture in their minds. They should not create eyestrain! Too much detail or small print forces your audience to hunch forward and squint to read all the text or numbers.

This chapter focuses on the design and layout options presented to you with most business presentation software. First, I outline the basics of design. I offer suggestions for creating different types of formats for your visuals, providing help on layout when you need to vary some of your pages, sometimes using graphics and sometimes only text. Even if you are an experienced presenter with a bag full of visuals already packed, you may find interesting new techniques in these pages.

Most business presenters haven't had a design or art class since college, if then. The concepts of design and placement of text and graphics are relatively new. Without boring you with too many design details, I give you a cram course on just those elements important to creating good visuals for presentations.

FINDING THE GRAPHIC DESIGNER INSIDE YOU

The graphic design process shows up everywhere. All the books and magazines, advertising, TV commercials—virtually everything we come in contact with that is printed or communicated—have been carefully designed. The commercials you view on TV and the books you read have been designed with you, the consumer, in mind.

Designers want to persuade, influence, entertain, inform, and educate. They want to make a direct connection to both the thinking side and the emotional side of your brain. You may not be able to identify a particular typeface in a book—but do know whether it is easy to read. Good design never gets in the way of the author's message.

Good design also helps communicate a message by attracting an audience and keeping their attention. Everyone is a designer—in one way or another. Besides choosing the words to use in your presentation, you make design decisions on the size and position you want those words to be in your visuals. You also decide the color of your background and whether to add any graphics. Each of these decisions affects your audience's perceptions of you and your message.

Think for a minute about something that caught your eye or kept your attention. What was it about the ad, billboard, or TV commercial that made you remember it? Was it the use of certain color combinations or an interesting typeface? Did a splash of humor or an especially poignant picture grab you? Think about these things and then consider whether there is anything you can use from what you see around you, and how you can incorporate these ideas into your presentation. If you begin to look at communication with the eyes of a graphic designer, you'll find a whole new creative spark inside, just waiting to get out.

Researchers have tried to come up with a magic formula for capturing the attention and interest of an audience. Much has been written about the techniques. In the following sections, we'll pass along some of the experts' tips.

FIRST, THE BASICS: PAGE LAYOUT

You should create a basic design standard for your visuals. Although you don't want every page to look the same, each page should conform to a standard. For example, you should choose where the title for each page will be placed, as well as the basic format of text, graphics, pictures, bullets, and so on.

Figure 5-1 shows a recommended visual layout guide for the title page and a bulleted list. The title page has two lines, one for the main title and one for the subtitle. You should center the text on these lines for best effect. The layout for the bulleted list page shows a centered title located in the top one-fourth of the page followed by a boxed bulleted list. The title is centered, but the bulleted list is left-justified. Choose a consistent bullet style and color.

You should also plan the layout for pages that contain other information, such as pictures or graphics. Figure 5-2 shows the basic page design. Notice that the graphic appears on the left side of the page. That may seem a little unusual, but placing it there has some interesting effects. People react positively to information presented with a picture on the left and text on the right, according to Ned Hermann, chairman of The Whole Brain Corporation. Hermann, recognized as

Page Layout: Title and Bulleted List

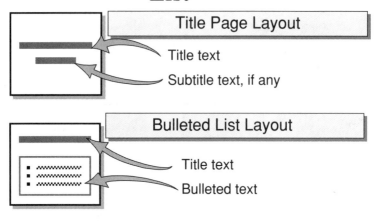

Figure 5–1 Recommended visual layout for a title page and bulleted list in a presentation

Page Layout: Text/Graphics

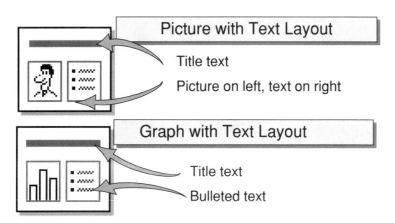

Figure 5–2 Placing graphics to the left of text makes your audience more interested in the presentation

Page Layout: Table, Columns, Organizational Chart

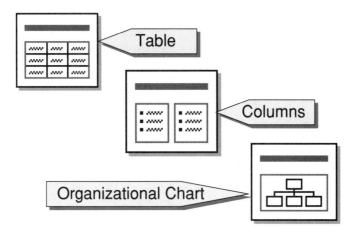

Figure 5–3   Sample layout pages

the father of brain dominance theory, studied the effects of using text and graphics for years. He found that proper placement of graphics helps wake up the audience and drives home communication—the audience retains more of what they see.

Your presentation may also include other visual elements, such as side-by-side columns, organizational charts, or tables. Plan the layout for these pages so that they'll have a consistent appearance. For example, Figure 5-3 shows sample layout pages for a table, columns, and organizational chart. Notice that the title line on each page appears in the same place, and that the margins on the top and the sides are consistent.

CHOOSING YOUR BULLETS WISELY

There is absolutely no end to the creativity you can use when selecting a bullet point for your presentation. In fact, the selection is so varied, many novice presenters find themselves overwhelmed by the sheer number of them.

Figure 5-4 shows the 223 symbols that make up the Wingdings typeface, which comes with Windows 3.1. With most presentation software packages, you can easily choose any character from this typeface. Choose your bullet styles wisely, especially if you are preparing a long presentation. While a clever bullet, such as a smiley face, may be cute here and there, it grows old when your audience sees it again and again.

You also have the option of using a small version of any clip art in place of a standard bullet. This is not recommended, however, since most presentation software packages will not automatically place the custom bullets you create using clip art. Manually placing your own bullets on a visual is no fun, and it adds up to a lot of work on long presentations. So find a bullet that you like from the characters available from a standard typeface, or from Wingdings.

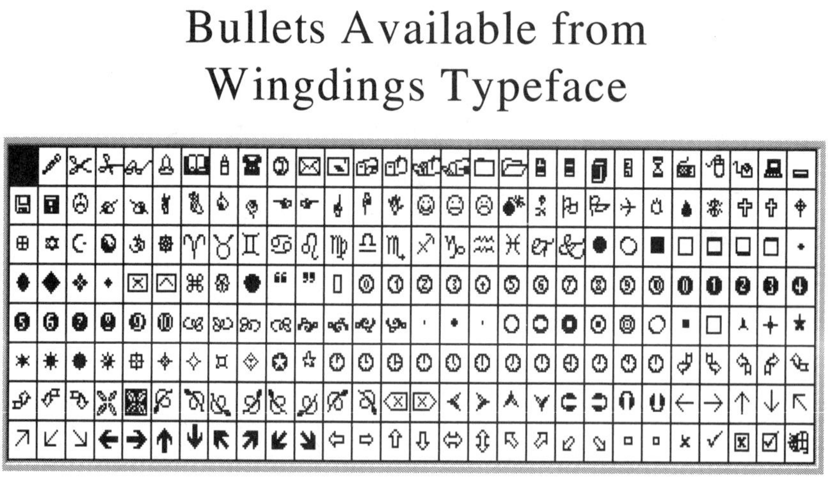

Bullets Available from
Wingdings Typeface

Figure 5–4   The 223 characters you can select from the Wingdings typeface

Table 5-1 shows several popular bullet options and their effects on a presentation. Make sure you try out your bullet selection on several types of visuals before you get too far along in the production of your presentation. Depending on your software, it may be difficult to make changes later in the process.

Table 5–1   Popular Bullet Options

Symbol	Type	Effect in Presentations
●○	Circle, ellipse	Works well in any type of presentation; makes a conservative statement; doesn't become boring after repeated use in long presentations. Watch bullet size in relation to text; keep it small so it won't overpower the text.
◆ ❖	Diamond	Works well in most presentations; less conservative than a circle or an ellipse; tends to make a point. Keep the size consistent with the text being introduced.
■ □	Square, rectangle	Sure bet for conservative presentations; unobtrusive. Keep square bullets small.
➜ ➔ ➢ ⇨ ↗ ◎ ⊃	Arrow	Reinforces the point of the text; arrows point out and up. Use straight, horizontal arrows that point to the text or arrows that point up (but not down) at text to convey an optimistic feeling. Don't use on slides with more than four lines of bulleted text.
◉ ◎	Target circle	An aggressive bullet that says each point is on target. Don't use on slides with more than four lines of bulleted text.
⊠ ✗ ☑	Checked box	Another aggressive bullet; really draws audience's attention. Don't use on slides with more than four lines of bulleted text.

USING BULLETED LISTS FOR MAXIMUM EFFECT

Pay careful attention to what comes after your bullet point—namely, the text. Visuals usually work best with only a few words, not full sentences; you want your audience to pay attention to you and not get distracted by reading lengthy text on the screen. Most people cannot read and listen well at the same time.

Some general rules for your bulleted text:

Keep text items short—use only a few key words or phrases. People read words one at a time when reading long sentences, but will read a short phrase as several words together. For example, the bulleted item, "Recommended Security Measures," can be read in one gulp, while the sentence, "The following six measures have been recommended by the board as better security measures," takes longer to read and understand.

Use no more than five bullets on a page. Pages with too many bulleted items will bore your audience. If you have a long list of topics, split them among several pages. To keep your audience focused, you may wish to use a numbered list rather than a bulleted one, especially if you want to convey a sequence of steps.

Use the same bullet shape for all points at the same level of importance (you can use different bullet symbols for the sub-points). Consistency and simplicity are key words here. Make sure your bullet points are consistent on each level. Also, if your presentation is likely to use several levels of topics and sub-topics, make sure that you use a plain bullet style. Figure 5-5 shows a page layout option from Microsoft's PowerPoint software with bullet points set at five levels.

Begin all bullet items with a similar style of wording—a noun or a verb, for instance, but not a mixture of both. For consistency's sake, start each bullet point on a list with the same type of word. Verbs work especially well. Consider the following points as an example: Developing the Strategy, Locating Team Members, Starting the Work, Obtaining Approvals. Starting each item with a verb gives the audience a sense that action is taking place.

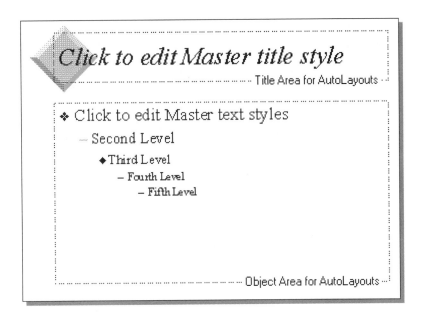

Figure 5–5   A master slide with bullet points set at five levels

Limit sub-topics to two or three items. Don't bore your audience with too many sub-points. If you keep to just two or three items, you'll avoid cramming too many details on a page.

Try to keep ideas on one screen. If your bulleted list must extend to multiple pages, let your audience know it. Either use ellipses (…) preceding the title or "(Continued)" following it to indicate clearly that the page is part of a longer list.

Keep your font consistent. Avoid varying your typeface on different levels of a bulleted list. It doesn't add anything to the look of your presentation and could confuse your audience. If you want to add emphasis, vary the point size or color of the text.

Choosing a Type Style

For the painter, there is the paintbrush; for the presenter, there is the typeface. You can use type to spruce up even the dullest presentation. Type is an especially powerful tool for conveying a message to the audience. Choosing the type size and typeface also sets the tone for your presentation.

As you work your way through the next few sections, use your own common sense and experience to determine what will work best for your audience. If you're not sure, take the conservative road. Luckily, many software packages today help you select the right typeface for a presentation. However, you should follow some guidelines on the use of type so that if you do modify a pre-cooked presentation style, you won't make a mess.

Typefaces

A *font* is a collection of letter shapes and numbers in one size, weight, and style—for example, 10-point Arial. A *type family* or *typeface* is a group of fonts in different sizes. All of the different Arial font sizes would constitute the Arial typeface. Depending on what kind of computer you have and which brand of software you use, the same font may have different names.

In Windows, the term *font* is used to mean a typeface. Typefaces are either serif or sans serif. Serif typefaces have "feet" on the bottoms and ends of the letters; sans serif fonts don't. Examples of serif typefaces are Times Roman, Courier, and Garamond—the font used in this book. Two sans serif typefaces are Arial and Avalon. Figure 5-6 shows the difference between serif and sans serif fonts.

As a general rule, serif fonts are considered more readable than sans serif fonts.

➤ Use a sans serif typeface for titles; this style is clean and easy to read even when the print is very large.

➤ Use a serif typeface for body text. It's easy to read, you can get more on a page, and serif type is legible even on a crowded page.

➤ Make the typefaces in the title and body text look distinctively different by adding bold or italics. Refrain from using ALL CAPITALS anywhere in your text or in your bullet points. If you wish to draw attention to a word or phrase, change the size of the type or put it in italics.

Serif versus Sans Serif

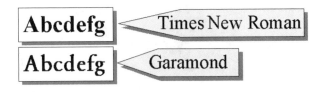

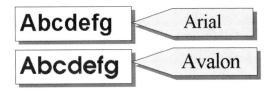

Figure 5-6   Examples of serif versus sans serif fonts. Times New Roman and Garamond are examples of serif fonts, while Arial and Avalon are sans serif fonts.

The bottom line on choosing a typeface is legibility—if you can't read it, don't use it. Also, you don't want the typeface to be the star of the show; it should enhance your message, not overshadow it.

Point Sizes

Socrates said, "If you stand for something important, write it in big, bold letters so that someone can see it." Clearly he knew a thing or two about making effective presentations.

Using upper- and lowercase type is important, since it provides a good focus for readability. Point size is very important too.

The *point size* of a font refers to the size of the letters. Type is measured in points and picas; there are 72 points to an inch. One pica is 12 points. Most presentation text for on-screen presentations should be a minimum of 24 points or larger. Titles should be 36 points or larger.

Table 5–2 Room Sizes and Corresponding Font Sizes

Room Size	Title Font Size	Text Font Size
Small conference room for 8 to 12 people	36-point	24-point
Mid-sized conference room for 12 to 40 people	40-point	28-point
Larger room for over 40 people	44-point	34-point

On the other hand, the type size must be small enough so that words can fit in the small area of the screen designated for them.

As a rule, make the point size bigger the farther it will be from your audience. If your presentation will take place in a large room with more than 30 people, increase the size of your font. Use Table 5-2 as a guide to recommended font sizes for different presentation settings.

▶ Note that for old-style overhead transparencies, you shouldn't use character point sizes smaller than 2.5 percent of the height of the image area. For example, if your screen is eight inches high (576 points), you should use at least a 14-point font (576 × 0.025). Naturally, if your presentation will be shown in a larger room with more than eight to ten people, you'll need to use larger fonts.

▶ For slides, you can judge the point size by holding the slide in your hand and trying to read it. If you can read the slide without having to use a slide viewer, the point size is okay. Regular text should be no smaller than one-twentieth the height of the chart for a computer screen, one-fiftieth for slides. Using a minimum 24-point text size for text and 36 points for titles will keep you out of trouble.

Text Alignment

Text can be flush left, flush right, left- or right-justified, or centered. Flush left is the most common format for text and bulleted lists, because people in Western countries usually start reading in the upper-

Alignment Example: Bulleted List

Left Alignment	*Centered Text*
•Know your audience	•Know your audience
•Set a plan of action	•Set a plan of action
•Get a professional coach	•Get a professional coach
•Check out equipment	•Check out equipment
•Rehearse often	•Rehearse often

Right Alignment
•Know your audience
•Set a plan of action
•Get a professional coach
•Check out equipment
•Rehearse often

Figure 5–7   Bulleted items look best when aligned flush left.

left corner and continue down the paragraph until they reach the bottom-right corner. Keep this in mind when you arrange your text placement; place the more positive information in the upper-left corner of the screen.

Stick to one alignment style—flush left, ragged right usually works best. Stay away from special styles (bold, underlining, and italics) unless you need to call attention to something specific. You may want to vary alignment techniques according to the type of text you are working with. For example, bulleted lists look best flush-left, but sometimes can be centered. Figure 5-7 shows a bulleted list aligned three different ways.

Paragraph text can also be centered, justified, or right- or left-aligned. The most common format for presentations is flush left, one of the examples shown in Figure 5-8. Notice how some alignment techniques—namely justified and right-aligned—leave gaping holes

Alignment Example: Paragraph

Centered	Justified Text	Right-aligned	Left-aligned
Use pie charts to show parts of a whole. The pie is divided into sections. The total of all sections equals 100%.	Use pie charts to show parts of a whole. The pie is divided into sections. The total of all sections equals 100%.	Use pie charts to show parts of a whole. The pie is divided into sections. The total of all sections equals 100%.	Use pie charts to show parts of a whole. The pie is divided into sections. The total of all sections equals 100%.

Figure 5–8   Examples of differently aligned text. Justified text often leaves extra spaces between words.

between words. This problem is common when the computer has to force words into tight margins.

Headings

Don't capitalize headings unless you feel you can't add EMPHASIS any other way. Better yet, try to make a practice of using a larger point size, boldface, or italics when you need to call out a word or heading. Usually when something is in all caps, people have trouble reading it. They sometimes feel like your visuals are "shouting" at them.

Tests have shown that all-capital text is also harder to read, especially in body text. For example, after conducting a study of its logo several years ago, Continental Airlines found that its all-uppercase, sans serif font wasn't as readable as a serif font was. So the company changed their logo from **CONTINENTAL** to Continental.

You can see the difference. Changing the font and adjusting from all uppercase to upper- and lowercase text made the company name much easier to read.

Some people read word by word; most can grasp phrases and lines if there aren't too many words on the line. Word recognition depends on the shape of the letters. Imagine drawing a line around a word and looking at the shape. Since the size of mixed upper- and lowercase types varies from character to character, the shapes of words differ, making word recognition easier. Words in all capitals, on the other hand, form a rectangular shape that is difficult to read. All-capital words also take up more space (up to 30 percent more) because they are taller and wider.

Finally, headings do not have to be centered on the screen. This is the traditional, newspaper-style method, but it does not lend itself to the way people read. Use your own taste when it comes to centering the text of headings and subheadings. You will most likely decide to center the titles and left-justify your bullet points.

Adding Interest with Color

With today's computer graphics, it is possible to select from hundreds of colors in a presentation. Why use color?

➤ To draw attention to a certain point on the screen

➤ To emphasize a single point on each visual

➤ To make emphasized points more vivid

➤ To prioritize items—people look at the brightest items first

➤ To make new points in a presentation

➤ To symbolize action: green for go, red for stop

➤ To suggest a mood (orange for good news)

➤ To build to a climax; start with darker shades and work up to lighter ones at the end of the presentation

Color and Mood

What is the right color of text and visuals for a presentation? It depends on the audience and the message. People react differently to various colors and color combinations. Sometimes people don't see color at all. According to research, eight percent of males and one percent of females have color-impaired sight (green and red are usually the problem colors). But for the rest of the population—the vast majority of your audience—color counts! It is another tool you can use to communicate to your audience.

Whatever shades you use, be consistent in your color scheme. It's okay to change your background color—to show a change to a new subject, for example—but try to stay in the same family of hues. Start with the darkest color and work toward paler shades.

Be sensitive to your audience. Remember that for many people, colors evoke not only a mood, but an era. Don't use colors that are out-of-date or old-fashioned. For example, using olive green and harvest gold may remind some people of kitchen appliances in the 1970s. It may send them into an emotional mood that you'd rather avoid.

Be sensitive to cultural biases as well. The colors pink and powder blue are nice, but they may not work for some audiences. Your audience may not interpret them as "serious" colors.

Base your colors on your audience, not your personal tastes. Avoid using large blocks of color, which tires the eyes. Red is the worst offender; it can be harsh and hard on the eyes.

"Warm" and "Cool" Colors

"Warm" colors are brighter and more dynamic than cool colors. They appear to advance to the viewer, implying foreground. Use red, yellow, or orange to imply depth and separation from the background. Warm colors represent action, closeness, and fun.

Yellow is the best color for visibility, followed by orange, vermilion, and yellow-green (imagine a pair of '70s bell-bottom pants or a neon poster). Honest, they work great! Schools use these colors because they seem cheerful and active, youthful and vibrant.

"Cool" colors appear to recede into the distance, offering stability. Greens and blues make good background colors. Cool colors can indicate status, background information, tragic or romantic situations, or efficiency and hard work. These colors create a quiet and relaxing mood. Avoid using bright shades of purple as a background; it is too vibrant and hard on the eyes. Keep in mind the lighting conditions of the room when choosing the shades for your background.

Beware of Blue

Despite the fact that blue is a favorite color for graphic artists, heed a few warnings. As a rule of thumb, you can't go wrong with blue for *backgrounds*. In fact, blue is such a great color for backgrounds that some presenters think it is good for any part of a visual. It isn't. Often blue flops when people try to use it for text, graphics, or pictures. Sometimes pale shades of blue don't photocopy well. If you have to make copies of a handout with blue text or graphs, you may be in trouble.

Also, blue letters can get lost on a page. Never use blue letters with a colored background unless you test how the result looks with every type of output device that you might some day use. What looks okay on your computer screen might be unreadable when projected on a big screen. Projection devices, color printers, and slide-making equipment all interpret colors a little differently. Hence, beware of blue. It can be a deceptive color if you use it for anything other than a background.

The Impact of Color

Researchers have done studies on how people react to colors, with fascinating results. A color may symbolize something in one culture but mean something entirely different in another. For example, in Western cultures people wear black to show that they are in mourning; in China, they wear white. What color you choose depends on your audience and your message.

In a survey done by the University of West Florida on political posters, black text on a yellow background was selected as the most legible color combination, though yellow was less popular than red, blue, and green. Black-on-blue and red with green were the combinations found to be least legible and least liked. We associate certain colors with holidays—red and green for Christmas, orange and black for Halloween, red-white-and-blue for July 4th. Avoid these color combinations unless you want your audience to think of those holidays.

When a color is part of a common expression, such as "in the red," using it can help you reinforce the idea.

The meaning and purpose of using color can change significantly from one type of audience to another. Ever wonder why some sugar packets sell well? Blue means sweet to some people. Blue is also often thought of as a conservative, "corporate" color. Blue means reliability to financial types, who associate it with authority, respect, and loyalty. However, to doctors, it may mean death. Dark blue can convey a sense of stability, maturity, and calmness. Light blue might be considered youthful, masculine, or cool.

If you're not sure which shade best suits the mood of your presentation, follow the suggestions from your software package. Most presentation software packages give you templates with preselected colors. Trained graphics artists conjure up those color combinations, so you generally can't go wrong.

Also, you may want to stick with your company's corporate style manual if one exists. You may not want to stray too far from those guidelines, especially for top-level presentations.

If you must select your own colors, Table 5-3 shows a list of colors and what they symbolize to some viewers. Keep in mind that this is only a starting point for thinking about color choices.

Table 5–3 Subjective Interpretations of Color by Different Audiences

Color Hue	Movie Audience	Financial Managers	Health Care Professionals	Control Engineers
Blue	Tender	Corporate, reliable	Dead	Cold, water
Cyan	Leisurely	Cool, subdued	Cyanotic, deprived of oxygen	Steam
Green	Playful	Profitable	Infected, bilious	Nominal, safe
Yellow	Happy	Highlighted item, important	Jaundiced	Caution
Red	Exciting	Unprofitable	Healthy	Danger

Table 5–4 Effect of Color Combinations

Color	Effect in Combinations
Yellow	Warm on white, harsh on black
Blue	Warm on white, hard to see on black
Red	Bright on white, warm or difficult to see on black
Yellow	Fiery on red, soothing on light blue

Color Combinations

If you aren't sure what colors work together, just look around. Look at print and TV advertising. What do their colors do for you? What buttons do they press? The human eye perceives colors in the foreground differently, depending on the background. Table 5-4 lists some combinations.

CHARTS AND GRAPHS

Charts and graphs give meaning to numbers and show the relationship between elements. They communicate information visually more quickly than raw data ever could.

Table 5-5 suggests what type of chart you should use to convey the type of information you have.

Table 5–5 Applications of Charts

Type of Chart	Best Application
Line charts	To represent information that changes over time, trends
Bar and column charts	To compare individual points of information, magnitudes
Pie charts	To show proportions such as sales by region, shares
Flow charts	To diagram processes
Organizational charts	To show reporting relationships in a hierarchy

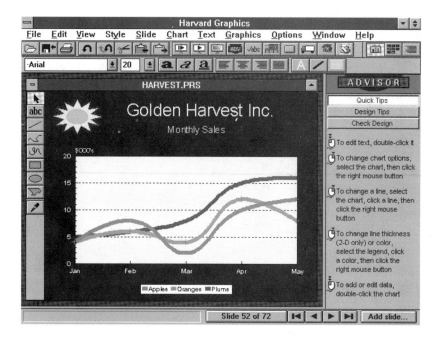

Figure 5-9 A line chart created in Harvard Graphics for Windows

Line Charts

Line charts are the best way to communicate ongoing events, such as sales or shipments over time. They communicate data on two scales: the y-axis scale shows the difference in data element values while the x-axis scale usually measures time.

Line charts clearly illustrate trends and statistics. Use grid lines and reference points to make the graph more readable. Minimize grid lines by using lighter shades or dot patterns that float behind solid areas. Figure 5-9 shows a classic line chart.

Bar and Column Charts

Column and bar charts are among the most common visuals used by business presenters. They are easy to create and quickly communicate a message when used to compare size, volume, or other tangible measure-

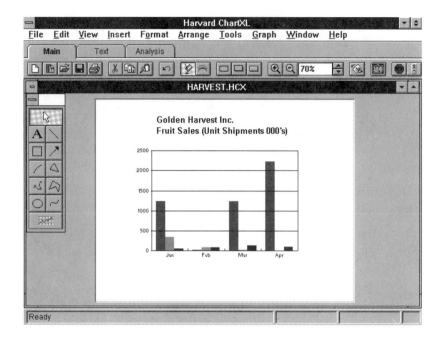

Figure 5-10   A column chart created in Harvard Graphics for Windows

ments. Sometimes a column chart communicates data faster, conveying a mass of information at once.

For example, charts plotted against the *x* and *y* axes can show change over a period of time. The *x* axis, or *time,* can proceed from left to right or from the bottom of the screen to the top (in a vertical chart). To show relationships or comparisons, bars can be stacked on top of each other (in a horizontal chart). Distinguish bars by using solid shades of color or simple patterns. Limit bars to five or fewer for each set of information you display. Figure 5-10 shows a classic column chart.

Pie Charts

Use pie charts to show the size of various parts that make up a whole unit, such as an annual budget. The "pie" is divided into sections, which, totaled together, equal 100 percent. Pie charts let the audience quickly see what slice makes up the largest piece of the pie. Limit pie charts to no more than five pieces, and only pull one piece out (this is called an *exploded slice*) if you need to for emphasis. Avoid adding depth to the chart. Many presentation programs let you convert your chart to a 3-D view, which gives thickness to the pie pieces or to bars in a bar chart. Unfortunately, this tends to distort the size of the wedges. As you can see in Figure 5-11, the bottom pie chart seems to show that hydrogen is the largest wedge. In the top pie chart you see that nitrogen is actually the largest slice of this pie.

Flow Charts

Flow charts provide an excellent way to visualize the relationship among *processes* rather than numbers. Flow charts support many of today's management practices, such as total-quality management and reengineering, because they create a picture of how work takes place.

Flow charting is a science; decision points, processing, creating files, and other activities are each represented by different symbols. You can choose to use a specific flow-charting tool or special symbol software depending on your needs for accuracy and updating. Most flow charts can be easily captured and added to your presentation files (see Figure 5-12).

Organizational Charts

Organizational charts show relationships among people, such as employees in a business. You can even plot a family tree with an organizational chart.

Most organizational charts used in business show the person's name, title, and sometimes a brief job description. The lines between the charts show reporting relationships and authority. Generally, the level of the box indicates a person's rank within the organization.

Many software packages contain an organizational charting feature. If you only have a small workgroup to chart, then a nonsophisticated utility usually works fine. If, however, you need to chart the lines of authority for a large organization, you should look for a stand-alone package dedicated to organizational charts. Most organizational

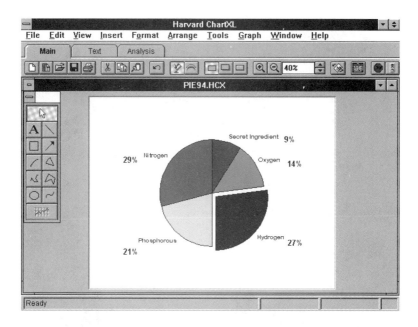

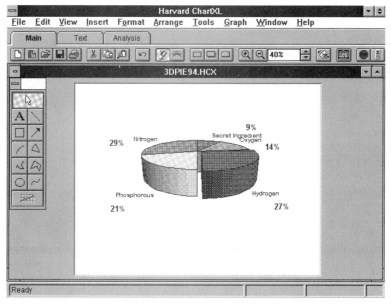

Figure 5–11 An exploded pie chart created in Harvard Graphics for Windows (top). Notice how the 3-D view distorts the relative size of the pie wedges (bottom).

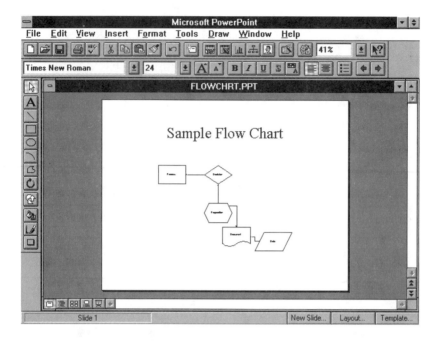

Figure 5–12 A flow chart created in Microsoft PowerPoint

charts can be pasted or transferred into your presentation as objects, as shown in Figure 5-13.

SETTING THE APPROPRIATE PACE

Appropriately placed pictures or clip art can drive home a point or elicit emotion. It helps members of your audience—especially creative, right-brained people—absorb your message much faster. But not all people will respond to the pace of your presentation in the same way.

For example, a three-year study by MediaNet, a New York City computer graphics firm, revealed that people near the age of 30 have a shorter attention span than those closer to 60. Thirty-year-olds grew up with electronic media and visuals; they don't want to sit through an overhead presentation with dull visuals. They want quickly-changing, full-color visuals such as slides and computer-based presentations.

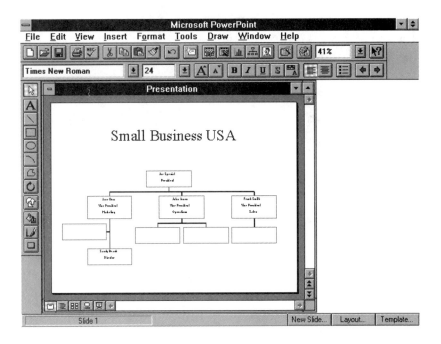

Figure 5-13 An organizational chart created in Microsoft PowerPoint

People between the ages of 45 and 60 also prefer color visuals, but delivered more slowly. Classic overhead projections and slides are appropriate for this generation. However, this group is also receptive to presentations with more sound and animation.

BECOMING A DESIGN EXPERT

This chapter touched on the major design concepts. As a business presenter you don't have to be a professionally trained graphic artist, but it does help to understand the basics. To help you create professional-looking visuals, you can rely on the sophistication found in presentation software. Like the old saying, "If you're not an expert, you ought to know someone who is." You can aptly rephrase it, "If you're not an expert, get software that is."

The next chapter offers a view of what is available in presentation software packages. The options today are exciting. Software developers have done a great job of making these programs easy to use—and smart, too.

Essential Tools and Technologies

Computers have become indispensable tools for business presentations. Automated tools turn the basic functions of creating, storing, and retrieving information into a simple process.

In fact, these days business professionals don't question the value of using a computer. The real question is, what software should you use with it? Chances are good you will use many different programs to create a presentation, from word-processing packages to research software, paint programs, clip art, and maybe even video and sound-mixing programs. Each one has its merits and uses.

Word-processing programs can be used to start your original outline, or prepare quick bullet charts. Many word-processing programs include the ability to combine graphics, either from a spreadsheet program or from within the word processor in your document. You can even print out the characters in different sizes and colors.

However, there is a special breed of programs created specifically to simplify the process of presentation preparation, production, and delivery. These are called presentation graphics programs.

This chapter discusses the options and opportunities available in presentation software. It covers the major features of this specialized class of software and the merits of the leading packages. If you haven't already selected a package, this chapter should help you sort through the features and understand the promises and pitfalls of various brand names.

First, a warning: Presentation software takes a lot of computing resources. Be sure to equip your computer with enough memory and disk space. Using presentation graphics software can be great fun, but trying to use it on a poorly equipped system is a slow and frustrating experience.

WHAT IS PRESENTATION SOFTWARE?

Business graphics once meant bar charts and graphs that were printed on a dot-matrix printer. Today's presentation software allows you to incorporate text, sound, animation, and video as well as charts and graphs. You can display the results on the computer screen or use a number of other different devices, including special computer projection panels, slides, and color printers.

The most important feature of a good presentation program (for non-professional designers) is the template. A *template* is a guideline with fonts, colors, and backgrounds already set up. Most software packages that come with templates have been created by talented graphic designers who carefully constructed the layout. All you have to do is put in the content.

Presentation software also allows you to do the following:

▶ Deliver an on-screen show with special effects
▶ Create other visuals, such as slides or overhead transparencies
▶ Prepare a variety of handouts
▶ Organize speaker's notes or prompts

▶ Create a "run-time" version, which lets you distribute copies of your presentation to others who may not have the presentation program

▶ Create charts, graphs, and tables

▶ Follow an outline or timeline

I compare various presentation packages throughout this chapter, including PowerPoint (Microsoft Corp.), Charisma (Micrografx, Inc.), Freelance Graphics (Lotus Development Corp.), Astound (Gold Disk), Aldus Persuasion (Aldus Corp.), WordPerfect Presentations (Novell/WordPerfect Corp.), and Harvard Graphics (Software Publishing Corp.).

SELECTING SOFTWARE: WHAT TO LOOK FOR

According to a market study conducted by System Research Corporation, people who use presentation software want a product that helps them create the most professional-looking presentation. They want an eye-catching show that gets results. They want a product that's intuitive and offers a quick learning curve. Buyers also want instant gratification; they want to learn the product quickly, then produce great-looking visuals. They want quick access to features and options without having to hunt through a complex maze of menus, and they want to complete a task in as few steps as possible.

I have studied the features of most of the presentation software packages on the market, compiling a list of seven feature areas and one other special consideration to consider when buying presentation software. I believe your decision to purchase a presentation package should be based on the following:

▶ **Ease of use.** How fast can you prepare a basic presentation?

▶ **Presentation templates.** Are there samples of presentations to use as examples? How easy are they to use?

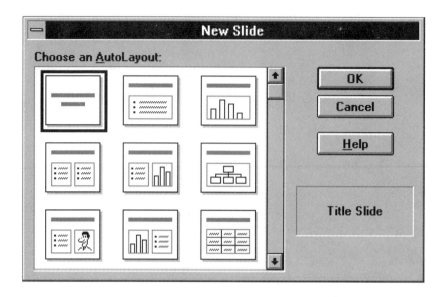

Figure 6–1   PowerPoint's AutoLayout feature contains place holders
                  for titles, text, and objects.

▶ **"Smart" tools.** Does the software offer help with designing or
  creating presentations? Does it have cue cards, "wizards," or
  "advisors" that look at your work and suggest better ways to
  create your presentation? (See Figure 6-1.)

▶ **Presentation formats.** What are the available output formats?
  Can you make speaker's notes and handouts for your
  audience easily? How easy is it to switch among or combine
  formats? Are transitions available?

▶ **Windows resources.** How well does the program run under
  Windows?

▶ **Charts.** Is there a chart feature in the program? How easy is it
  to create a chart and make changes to it? How easy is it to
  import or paste data or charts from a spreadsheet or other
  external program?

▶ **Graphics formats.** Does the software have good drawing tools? Can you import pictures from another source? Can you easily rearrange them? Does the software come with a good starter kit of business-oriented clip art?

Finally, another important consideration is the "local popularity poll." Check with some of your colleagues to see which software they use for making their presentations.

Why? Because you will likely share presentations. Over time, business presenters build up a large library of presentations. Often, members of a workgroup or business team share presentations. It can be a real time-saver simply to update or rework a presentation rather than start from scratch.

If your colleagues use a different software package than you do, however, borrowing won't be so easy. All presentation software packages use proprietary file formats, which make it difficult to transfer files from one package to another. Luckily, Windows makes it easy to cut and paste individual pages from one presentation to another. Still, the process isn't perfect; expect to spend time reworking the text and sometimes the color schemes.

BASIC FEATURES OF PRESENTATION PROGRAMS

When you go shopping for a software program, keep in mind what kind of presentations you want to make. If your needs are for simple visuals with a few charts and tables, then you will find a wide variety of software to choose from. In the following sections I'll describe a few features you should look for and the more popular programs that include them.

Organizing Your Presentation

You usually have two choices for arranging your presentation: outlines and templates. With an outliner, you create your presentation by

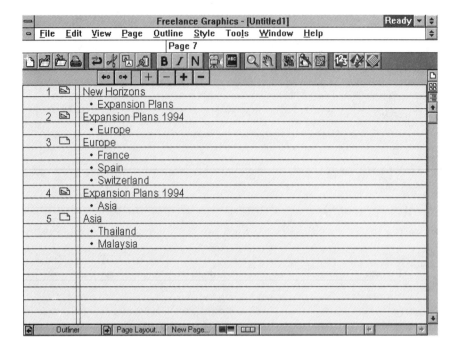

Figure 6–2   You can add and edit text or add, move, and delete
pages with Freelance Graphics' outline option.

typing an outline, which is translated into the format you have chosen
(usually bulleted text). The title of each screen appears with the bulleted items underneath it. This method is useful for checking the
content of your presentation.

Outlines

Many programs offer the ability to import text from a word processor—great if you need an outline, thesaurus, or grammar checker.

Freelance Graphics shows you text on a yellow legal pad (see
Figure 6-2). The outline is very similar to word-processor outlining. In
fact, you can paste an outline from Ami Pro, Word for Windows, or
WordPerfect for Windows, and Freelance Graphics will automatically

turn it into a basic presentation for you. Speakers' notes look like 3-by-5 index cards.

In the outline mode, you specify levels of text such as title lines, subtopics, and detail lines. You can specify different bullet symbols and formats for each level.

Most presentation programs also have a built-in spell-checker; however, you will still have to proofread your document, because the spell-checker doesn't catch all types of errors.

Other word processor–type features include editing; specifying the type size, font, and color; using automatic text wraps; and variable line and paragraph spacing.

Templates

Most presentation programs include a selection of predesigned templates. Templates format your presentation into screens, incorporating the background and logos into master screens. Changes to the master usually affect all screens on which they are based. All screens that contain a heading, a subhead, and bullets are based on the master screen.

For example, PowerPoint provides templates in five versions for each type of design: black-and-white overheads, 35-mm slides, speaker's notes, handout pages, and outline pages.

Freelance Graphics has SmartMaster presentation styles to choose from, as shown in Figure 6-3, as well as a SmartMaster Business Pack that contains additional SmartMaster sets and clip art symbols.

Embellishing Your Presentation

After you use an outline or template to create the basic structure of your presentation, you can use the following tools to add the supporting data and visuals that will strengthen your message.

Charts and Graphs

You can import either data or complete graphs into a presentation program. You type in data, usually in a spreadsheet format, select a chart style, and have the chart drawn for you by the program. Freelance

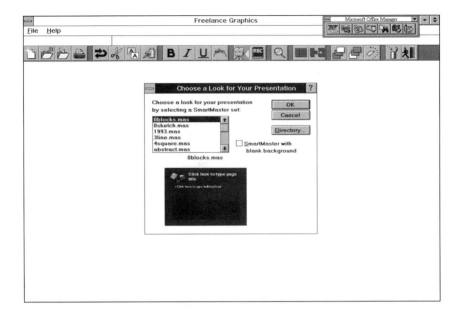

Figure 6–3   Freelance Graphics' SmartMaster controls the look with page layout, fonts, and colors.

Graphics has an extensive choice of bar, chart, and line graphs. You can preview graph styles before selecting one.

Harvard Graphics lets you use formulas in cells, like a spreadsheet. However, it falls short in designing organizational charts. The boxes in these charts are a fixed size. When you change or enlarge the text, the text boxes don't resize themselves to accommodate the change, so they can get pretty crowded—and look unprofessional.

PowerPoint's graph tools include OLE (object linking and embedding) applications such as Organizational Chart, Art Gallery, and Graph. Organizational Chart is the only application to date that allows shared reporting of positions. Art Gallery is a clip art manager. Graph (which uses lots of system resources, unfortunately) offers bar, chart, line, and scatter charts, as well as 3-D and donut charts, as shown in Figure 6-4.

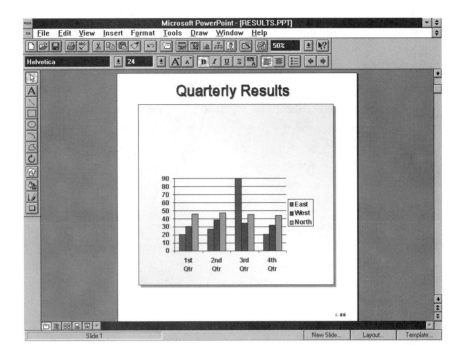

Figure 6–4   PowerPoint's chart gallery displays several different chart formats.

Simple Drawings

Most presentation software packages include drawing and manipulation tools to create boxes, circles, polygons, and lines. These objects can be filled with a single color or a gradient of different colors, as well as textures. Textures are patterns of lines, dots, or both. Other features include the ability to undo the last thing you did, to line up objects you created, and to group objects together (for moving and resizing).

Virtually all of the popular presentation software packages handle basic drawing functions. PowerPoint is probably the easiest to learn and the most intuitive. Harvard Graphics for Windows and Freelance Graphics also include many easy-to-use functions.

Clip Art

PowerPoint supplies a large collection of business clip art as well as a clip art manager so you can add your own favorite pieces. It also lets you group and ungroup clip art so you can create more custom pictures.

Micrografx Charisma, which comes from a publisher with excellent graphics software, gives you even more control of graphics pieces. It lets you fill an object with hatch patterns, tiled bitmaps, clip art symbols, photographic images, and types of gradients. Charisma even comes with a clip art-filled CD-ROM.

Harvard Graphics and Freelance Graphics also come with clip art. If you create a lot of visuals in your presentations, you may wish to supplement the clip art that comes with your software by buying a clip art library. That way you get thousands of images that you can paste easily into your applications. See Appendix B for a list of vendors with clip art libraries.

"Smart" Software

One of the interesting new features found in presentation software are improved tutorial and help systems. "Help" doesn't just mean assistance on how to use commands. Harvard Graphics has an "advisor" feature that offers Quick Tips and Design Tips.

PowerPoint's AutoContent Wizard, shown in Figure 6-5, asks you a few questions about your presentation and offers you a set of four steps that form the basis for your presentation. There are basic presentation types, from selling a product to recommending a strategy. Each screen includes a heading and instructions on the type of text or chart to add. You replace the text and charts with your own creation.

The Pick-a-Look Wizard helps you determine how you want your presentation to look by guiding you through a series of steps. You pick the type of presentation, a master template, and whether you want screens, speaker's notes, handouts, and outline pages.

Freelance Graphics' QuickStart tutorial, shown in Figure 6-6, teaches you how to use Freelance Graphics to create presentations. The series of demonstrations and practice sessions are easy to follow.

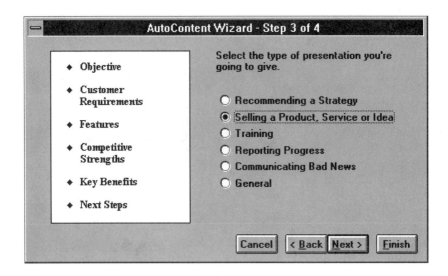

Figure 6–5 PowerPoint's AutoContent Wizard

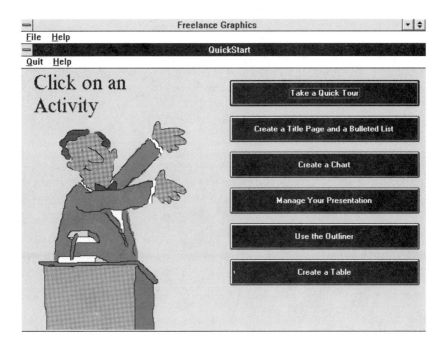

Figure 6–6 Freelance Graphics' QuickStart feature is an interactive, on-line tutorial.

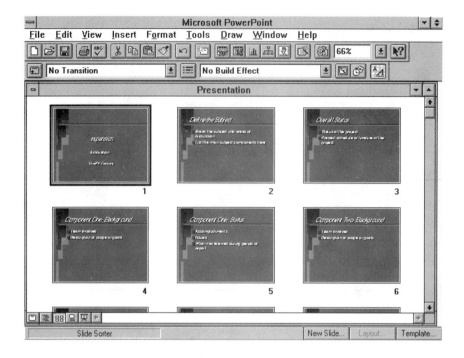

Figure 6–7   PowerPoint's slide sorter is like working with slides on a light table, only you won't strain your back.

Slide Sorters and Editors

In the old days, you had to either hold your slides up to a light or use a light table to view the slides in the order that you were going to project them. It wasn't too comfortable squinting your eyes or staring into the bright light. A computer-based slide sorter, available in most presentation packages, lets you see slide-like icons that represent all the screens, arranged in the order of the presentation. This is referred to as viewing a "thumbnail" of your screens (see Figure 6-7). Changing the order of a slide is easy. Just drag the thumbnail on the screen to a point earlier or later in the presentation.

PowerPoint allows you to annotate your screens. Harvard Graphics lets you open up to four presentations at once and cut-and-paste screens among them. Charisma lets you add layers of objects and effects to your screens. Layers are useful for segregating different objects that appear together. That way, you can work on an object without affecting the other elements on the screen.

Delivery

Presentation programs usually have the ability to display on-screen shows. Some, like PowerPoint and Harvard Graphics, permit drawing on the presentation during a show. Most provide a run-time player, which lets you distribute a copy of your presentation for others to see, even if they don't have a copy of the presentation software.

Harvard Spotlight from Software Publishing Corporation is a software application that enables users to organize, rehearse, and deliver their existing electronic presentations more effectively. The product is built around the concept of a customizable Presentation Desktop, displaying up to seven windows suited to a user's specific needs. While the audience views the current screen in a presentation, the presenter can monitor and control any of the following information: current screen on display, presentation notes, next-screen preview, and timing and pacing information—all on a VCR-style navigation bar.

Special Effects

The newer presentation programs let you incorporate some multimedia features: sound, animation, and video. Usually this is done by inserting an "object" into your slide, just as you would insert clip art. Depending on the software, you can also place an on-screen button over your sound or video object so you can play it at will during the presentation.

Most programs include some transition effects as part of their screen-show features. A *transition effect* determines the way a screen show proceeds from one screen to another. Pushing one slide away with another, fading in from black, or dissolving from one slide to another are examples of transitions. Presentation software packages usually include different screen show transition effects, including dissolves, wipes, and fades.

Some programs also let you display a bulleted list one item at a time. This is an effective way to introduce topics and subtopics.

Handouts

When preparing handouts, consider how your presentation looks on paper. Most business presentations require some form of handout for the audience. Your presentation software likely gives you print options that specifically make your handouts look good in black and white, even if your presentation contains lots of colors and busy backgrounds. Check the Print feature of your software to see what your options are.

Most likely you will need a high-resolution printer (like an HP LaserJet) that prints at least 300 dots per inch (dpi). If you have pictures, photos, clip art, or intricate graphics, try to use a higher-resolution printer, one at 600 dpi. (See the sections on printers later in this chapter.)

Some programs like PowerPoint, shown in Figure 6-8, allow you to print out handouts to go with your presentation. Freelance Graphics

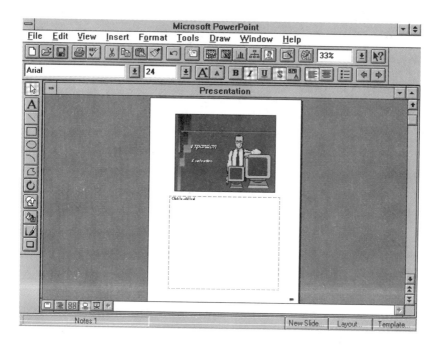

Figure 6–8   PowerPoint prints handouts to support your presentation.

lets you produce both speaker and audience handouts, as well as handouts with up to six screens per page.

Quick-Reference Guide to Useful Software

Obviously there is a lot of helpful software available. In the following sections I'll describe the packages I believe are especially flexible and easy to use.

Presentation Software

The following packages support the basic features of good presentation programs and allow you to prepare a presentation quickly and without too much fuss. For more information on the manufacturers and where to find this software, see Appendix B.

Charisma

Charisma (Micrografx, Inc.) has features found in multimedia authoring, paint, and drawing packages. You also get a clip art and multimedia library on CD-ROM. One of the great features of this program is its support of precise color control. The bitmap tools let you adjust color balance, brightness, and contrast.

If you are familiar with other Micrografx products, such as Designer, you'll feel right at home with Charisma. This program is not designed for novice users; if you aren't already familiar with presentation graphics or illustration programs, this is not the package for you.

Freelance Graphics for Windows

Freelance Graphics (Lotus Development) is an easy-to-use package for those who want a full-featured package with a minimum of fuss and maximum productivity.

The charting feature's data sheet shows you easily where to enter the data you're charting. It also displays graph components (bars or pie slices) in the same color as the associated rows and columns in your data sheet, so you can see exactly how your data are being graphed.

Freelance Graphics can be integrated with other Lotus programs, a feature that can save you a lot of time. For example, you can transfer information about your presentation into a Lotus Notes database or import Lotus 1-2-3 data for charting.

Harvard Graphics for Windows

Designed for the business presenter, Harvard Graphics (Software Publishing) is a good all-around package. An interesting feature is the Design Checker, which interactively checks your presentation against various design guidelines that have been developed by presentation experts.

For example, if you create a pie chart with eight slices, the Design Checker suggests that using six or fewer slices would improve the overall appearance and effectiveness of the chart. You can then switch to another chart type or combine some of your data to create fewer slices.

PowerPoint

PowerPoint (Microsoft) is easy to use and is available on both Macintosh and DOS platforms. This software has good notes and outline features. The AutoContent Wizard sets up a canned presentation with a bulleted list of topics you should cover, such as the background on the situation and vision for the future. Change the background with the Pick-a-Look Wizard, which walks you through the selection process for every visual aspect of your presentation.

The Rehearsal feature helps you fine-tune a presentation by keeping track of the time you spend on each slide and the total presentation time. You can also turn the presentation into a text document using the Report It tool.

Astound

Astound (Gold Disk) is available on both Mac and PC platforms. Presentation components—text, graphics, and charts—can become multimedia objects. Each object has a timeline associated with it on a screen.

If you want lots of sound or video clips, or need to incorporate animation, then Astound is your tool. One of its strongest features is its ability to synchronize multimedia objects.

Other Software You'll Need (or Want)

Beyond the basic presentation software, you may wish to put a few more packages in your toolbox. Software such as special drawing tools, supplemental clip art libraries, and presentation delivery software make it easier to construct the perfect presentation for all occasions.

Drawing and Graphics Tools

Most presentation software includes rudimentary drawing capabilities. Depending on your needs, however, you may want to add a few more tools to create custom drawings. For specific shapes, products like Micrografx' SnapGraphics, or Shapeware Corporation's Visio can give you a library of shapes—from triangles to squares to polygons (see Figure 6-9).

Charting Tools

If you work with complex data, you may need a dedicated charting tool to help analyze and communicate your information more effectively. Products such as Harvard ChartLX (Software Publishing), SigmaPlot (Jandel Scientific), Origin (MicroCal Software), and DeltaGraph (DeltaPoint Software) provide charting help above and beyond what's available in presentation or spreadsheet software.

For example, Harvard ChartLX lets you choose from hundreds of chart types geared toward business, statistical, or technical data. If you aren't a charting expert, you need look no further than the built-in Graph Gallery Advisor, a feature that gives you advice and recommendations. For example, the Advisor recommends using a spider plot for proportional comparisons and a bubble plot for comparative positioning.

Clip Art Libraries

One of the easiest ways to add life to an otherwise dull business presentation is through the use of appropriate clip art. A simple picture added

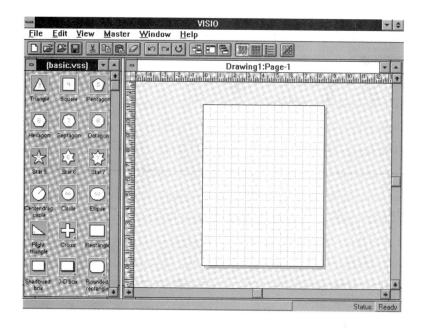

Figure 6–9   The left side of Visio's main screen shows all the shapes available for custom drawing.

to your visuals helps "wake up" your audience. It also provides graphic cues to the audience to help them follow your topic.

Many business presentation packages include a generous library of figures and clip art, as shown in Figure 6-10. But for the serious presenter, supplemental libraries are important. Libraries from Corel, Masterclips, Lotus Development's SmartPics, and others have especially useful art for the business presenter.

Delivery Software

Products such as SPC's Harvard Spotlight let you organize, rehearse, and deliver electronic presentations more effectively. They read the presentation files that you created with PowerPoint, Freelance Graphics, or Harvard Graphics. Then you can divide the presentation and show it on two PC screens—one for the presenter and one for the audience.

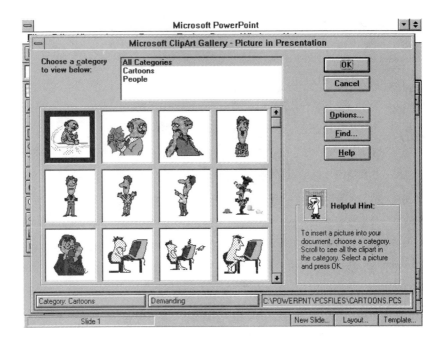

Figure 6-10   Microsoft PowerPoint comes with an extensive gallery of clip art.

The audience's screen shows the actual display of the presentation, while the other shows a special display for the presenter, which displays a preview of the next slide or lists any speaker's notes. You use it as other speakers use the TelePrompTer. The presenter's screen can also be used to display all the slides in the show, and you can rearrange them if a mid-course correction becomes necessary.

Harvard Spotlight also offers timing and pacing tools to help you plan the overall flow of a presentation. You can set the time for an entire presentation and automatically distribute the times across individual slides, or vary the time on a slide-by-slide basis. An on-screen ahead/behind "fuel gauge" flags you if you get too far ahead or behind in your presentation. Figure 6-11 shows a presenter's screen from Harvard's Spotlight.

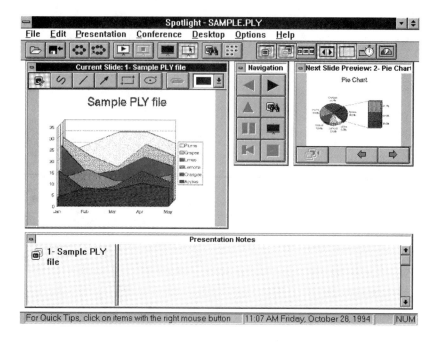

Figure 6–11   The presenter's screen in Harvard Spotlight. The current slide is on the left; the next slide in the presentation is on the right.

One caveat: This type of product is more complex to set up than a plain presentation package. It will take you a little extra time and effort to configure the equipment on the day of the presentation, but gaining control over the presentation, timing, and speaker's notes might just be worth it.

HARD FACTS ABOUT HARDWARE

Graphics programs consume computing resources like no other software. Some people call them "resource hogs"—and for good reason.

Computing resources like memory, processor time, and disk space can quickly be depleted if you use a lot of graphics, clip art, graphs, or pictures in your presentation. If you use scanned images, such as logos, photos, or other bitmapped files, you can quickly turn a presentation file from under 100,000 bytes to well over a million. Check the amount of free disk space on your computer before you load the presentation software. Most software programs take over 20 megabytes (20MB) of disk space. Clip art libraries easily consume another 40MB to 100MB. Plus each file that you create takes up still more space.

Sometimes just loading a program can eat up *system* resources—the amount of memory your computer can use during a work session. Toolbars, fonts, and other options make the software highly functional and easy to use, but these features do charge a price. For example, Charisma uses 13 percent of system resources on start-up and can quickly drag your system down. PowerPoint uses 15 percent at start-up and can easily use 18 to 54 percent of the system resources when you use programs that link or embed charts or graphic pictures into your presentation. Moreover, some programs fail to relinquish a part of memory when you close them. If your computer appears sluggish after you run presentation software, you may have to exit completely and restart the computer to gain all the resources back. Sometimes just restarting Windows will do the trick.

Moreover, you should be careful about reading the "minimum" configuration suggested by the software publisher. Often software publishers try to make their products look more attractive by lowering their recommended minimum configuration. Unfortunately, this does the user a disservice.

Table 6-1 lists minimum and recommended hardware configurations for basic business presentation software.

This equipment will serve adequately for developing most presentations, but it will fall short of your needs if you choose to develop multimedia presentations. (I'll talk more about the equipment needs for multimedia in Chapter 7.)

Presentation Gear You'll Need

If you've already started assembling a hardware shopping list, let me give you a few more items to add to it. Business presenters have special

Table 6–1 Hardware Recommendations for Basic Business
Presentation Software

Component	Minimum	Recommended
Computer CPU	486 chip, 50 MHz or higher	Pentium chip, 60 MHz or higher
RAM (memory)	8MB	16MB or more
Free hard disk space	100MB	200MB
Video	256-color VGA	16.7-million-color VGA
Printer (black and white)	300-dpi laser	600-dpi laser

requirements for everything from printers to pointing devices. Following are a few items to consider.

Black-and-White Printers

Almost all presentations will at some point require a black-and-white printer, whether to create handouts or for speaker's notes. For the most part, you'll want a printer that is capable of making clear, crisp copy. You have two items to consider when selecting a black-and-white printer: the resolution of the print and the printing language.

Standard 300-dpi laser printers usually suffice for simple handouts, but the better resolution of 600-dpi laser printers is helpful for most visuals. Printers in this category are generally under $1,000. If your visuals are very intricate or include photos, you may wish to use a 1,200-dpi printer.

You should also decide whether your printer needs to use the PostScript language or another printing language (such as the Hewlett-Packard standard PCL). Usually PostScript printers are a little more expensive but carry a standard set of fonts. Years ago, PostScript compatibility was very important for consistency of fonts, but it is not so crucial today.

The Hewlett-Packard line of LaserJet printers is the most popular for standard business presentations. Other low-cost laser printers that follow the Hewlett-Packard standard, such as models from Texas Instruments or Canon, are also popular.

Color Printers

You may wish to create your visuals in color for overhead transparencies or handouts. In either case, you'll want to choose a high-quality printer capable of creating crisp colors. There are several technologies used in color printers that affect price and quality.

Ink-jet printers are the least expensive and don't usually require special paper. Hewlett-Packard and Canon both make printers in this category. These printers work fine for handouts if you are preparing an informal business presentation. But try them out before you buy one; they may not match the quality you want if you are trying to project a very professional image.

Thermal printers, such as those from Tektronix, make much better quality printouts but usually require specially treated paper. Color laser printers are also available, but these printers are more expensive.

Innovations abound in the color printer category. For example, Fargo Electronics married two related color technologies, wax thermal and dye sublimation, to create one extremely flexible color output device. Both technologies create high-resolution color transparencies, and the dye sublimation produces photographic-quality output. Fargo also offers a line of low-cost printers.

Most color printers print slowly, less than a page per minute. If you have a large presentation or need many sets of copies, create one master copy on a color printer and then use a color copy machine to reproduce the rest.

LCD Projectors

Among the best innovations for business presenters are liquid-crystal display (LCD) projection panels, which let you present slide materials directly from a PC. These thin panels fit over a high-intensity overhead projector and hook up to the VGA (monitor) port of a computer, projecting anything that appears on your screen through the overhead.

Sometimes the quality of the projection is less than perfect, but it can be improved if you follow a few tips. First, make sure you use a high-intensity (very bright) overhead projector. Second, try to dim the lights in the front of the room. Third, adjust the color and focus carefully. Most projection panels have their own adjustment controls for screen size, contrast, tint, and sometimes focus.

Good-quality LCD projection panels are available from InFocus Systems, Sharp, nView, and other manufacturers.

Other On-screen Projectors

For large halls, you may have to equip yourself with a front- or rear-screen video projector. These projectors may contain one or three lights that take the VGA output from your computer and project it on a large screen; the projectors may be portable or permanently mounted onto the ceiling. Make sure you check the specifications for these projectors; some of the older ones do not handle standard VGA output very well and others have trouble with video feeds.

One of the more innovative products in this category is InFocus Systems' LitePro, which includes a projector, stereo speakers, and a multi-input, audio-video interface and active-matrix color LCD panel, which outputs 1.4 million colors with a 640×480 pixel resolution.

Barco, long known for its quality projector systems, produces an interesting three-gun projector called the Barcodata 701, a large-screen projector system for the PC. The projector is based around a three-gun system that is mounted on the ceiling. It can handle most PC graphic output, as well as a variety of TV and video formats.

TVs and Large Monitors

If you have a small audience, you can use a large-screen monitor or a TV set as an alternative to projection panels and projectors. Several vendors, such as NEC, Sharp, and Mitsubishi make computer monitors that measure 17 inches, 21 inches, or even 35 inches diagonally.

This rivals most TV screens and turns into a suitable format for conference room presentations. It is best to elevate the monitor to the height of the presenter or a little higher, so that the audience doesn't have to look up and down too much.

You can also try hooking up a regular large-screen TV. Consumer Technology Northwest offers a series of VGA-to-NTSC adapters, which translate the output of the computer into one that a TV can interpret. One model even offers sound capabilities. By plugging a microphone or telephone handset into a port, you can record your voice or audio sound effects without a conventional audio board.

Be sure to test this type of equipment with your computer to make sure everything is compatible. Once tested, however, you can carry along the adapter to create a portable multimedia spectacle.

Film Recorders

Making 35-mm slides has always looked like magic. Many business presenters prefer to use a slide-making service rather than go to the trouble of creating 35-mm slides in house. For those who want the freedom and control of the slide-making process, however, there are several alternatives.

Mirus Industries Corp.'s FilmPrinter turbo PC portable film recorders are simple to use and produce high-quality 35-mm slides from ordinary film for about 50 cents per slide. FilmPrinter requires no board installation, just a simple parallel-port attachment. Although the hardware is easy to set up, the software is a little confusing because it includes so many options. You can specify the film type, control the orientation and resolution, and even customize color tables.

Polaroid makes the Digital Palette CI-5000S which works well as a desktop film recorder. It works best for slides composed of straightforward text and line art. The device supports a variety of film types, including 35-mm slide film, 3×4–inch instant print film, 3¼×4¼–inch instant prints, and overhead transparencies.

Unfortunately, film recorders are notorious for their glitches and "gotchas." Sometimes they don't support certain types of graphics, like bitmapped images, and some don't support PostScript fonts. As with other high-tech solutions, make sure you test out the equipment carefully before you face a crunch deadline.

Pointing Devices

Business presenters have a choice of wireless pointing devices that, like wireless microphones, give you great freedom to travel around the room. Wireless pointing devices take the place of the computer mouse and work well with most presentation software.

They use either radio-controlled or infrared technology, but both technologies have their drawbacks. A radio-controlled mouse works well, but sometimes can suffer from interference with wireless microphones or other wireless devices in the immediate area. I know of one business meeting in a hotel in which the presenter couldn't get the wireless mouse to work because the same frequency was being used in another meeting two floors away.

Infrared devices don't suffer from signal interference, but sometimes they have a shorter range, and they always require a clear line of sight to the infrared controller. Still, these products provide great freedom and flexibility and are worthwhile tools.

Some wireless pointing devices act as more than a simple mouse clicker. For example, the Mind Path IR90 from Mind Path Technologies lets you control your computer from up to 60 feet away. Using infrared technology (the type used on remote-control TV devices), you can adjust the brightness, contrast, and position of the image on the LCD projection panel. The "mouse" has eight buttons that can be programmed for a numerical keyboard and Menu, Pause, and Esc buttons. You can also use the mouse to add check marks on the screen or to highlight a critical passage. It's great for drawing attention to key points.

The GyroPoint Remote, a radio-controlled device, from Gyration Inc. uses a radio link to communicate with the PC. The receiver, which is attached to a serial port, communicates with a transmitter that you can attach to your belt. You can manipulate an on-screen pointer by moving your wrist up, down, left, or right.

Tools for the Road

Business presenters should choose portable computer equipment carefully if they plan to take their presentations on the road. Luckily, over the last few years portable computers have become much more powerful and can be fully configured to deliver business presentations. The following checklist is recommended gear for taking your show on the road:

> ➤ Notebook or laptop computer with a minimum of 256-color VGA output; make sure your computer has a VGA port on the back (not all sub-notebook computers do)
>
> ➤ 250MB or larger hard drive
>
> ➤ Mouse port for hooking up an external mouse
>
> ➤ Serial connection for attaching a wireless mouse
>
> ➤ Parallel connection for printing
>
> ➤ AC power supply (don't depend on the computer batteries)
>
> ➤ Wireless mouse
>
> ➤ LCD projection panel (or other projector for on-screen presentations)

Be aware that portable computer technology changes rapidly. I've watched the innovations and evolution of portable computers since 1984, and one thing is clear: The technology changes every six months!

Most business presenters want top-of-the-line computers for road trips. Make sure you consider your own needs and that the portable you buy lives up to your expectations.

ONE MORE THING TO CONSIDER

By now you've probably created a big shopping list. You know the tools and technologies for almost any type of business presentation. But before you take off for the store, consider just one more technology: multimedia.

If you really want to add sparkle to your presentation, look at the options available with multimedia. In the next chapter, I introduce the newest generation of presentation packages. These add sound, animation, and video to your business presentation. Sound interesting? It is!

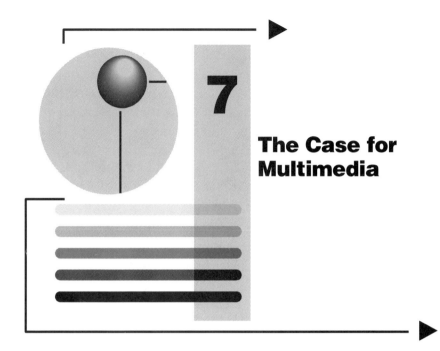

The Case for Multimedia

Pictures, motion, and sound. Add them up and what do you get? You can get an efficient and powerful way to communicate—especially today when we seem to be constantly inundated with information. By appealing to our various senses, multimedia can convey your message in a way that traditional methods cannot. More importantly, you can save time by driving home points more quickly.

According to a study J.D. Fletcher conducted for the Institute for Defense, the amount of time it takes to make a point can be reduced by 31 percent using multimedia and interactive learning. You can get the message through to an audience in far less time when you *show* them than you can when you simply *tell* them.

Most people agree that adding sights and sounds to your presentations helps make your point. But, you may ask, isn't it expensive or terribly difficult to do? On the contrary, the cost of training presentations can be reduced by 64 percent through the use of multimedia, according to the J.D. Fletcher study.

Consider the case of Steve McDowell. "Medicine changes overnight. And so can I," says McDowell, the owner of Sanchez Street Graphics, a producer of training tutorials for the medical field. McDowell creates training tutorials on medical procedures, which, he notes, change all the time. But thanks to his prowess with multimedia equipment, he can create a new tutorial in a couple of hours. He just uses a video camera to get over-the-shoulder pictures of procedures. Then McDowell uses an Intel Smart Video Recorder to edit the video clips, mixes them with other graphics, and creates an up-to-the-minute multimedia training presentation.

You may have heard or read about multimedia, but quickly dismissed it for your own presentations because you lacked the budget or specially trained staff to put together an intricate production for you. Well, take heart, because creating a stunning presentation with video and sound might just be easier and less costly than you think. Thanks to new technology, you'll find that great tools are available at a fraction of the cost they were just a few years ago.

This chapter introduces the idea of using multimedia for business presentations. It's a new concept, but it is also powerful—and surprisingly affordable. I start by defining the term *multimedia,* then relate it to how and why business presenters might use it. Then I turn briefly to some of the myths that surround multimedia and address some of the misconceptions that people commonly have. Finally, I dive into the details of what to use and how to use it. Even if you've dismissed the concept before, you may emerge from this chapter with a whole new perspective about multimedia's place in your next business presentation.

WHAT IS MULTIMEDIA?

If you need a textbook definition of multimedia, think of it this way: Multimedia is technology that combines the use of several media for communications. Usually it combines motion and sound. Sometimes it is referred to as the convergence of voice, video, text, and data.

For business presenters, multimedia often involves introducing both sound and some form of movement into a presentation. The additional media might come from video or from computer-generated graphics.

Efficient Training

The great promise of multimedia technology comes from its ability to enhance the way people communicate with each other and make a point. Professional trainers and communicators have long struggled with techniques for communicating messages in ways that make people more apt to remember what was said.

According to researchers, there's a cumulative effect when people use multiple senses to acquire knowledge. For example, people retain in short-term memory only about 20 percent of what they see, 40 percent of what they see and hear, and 70 percent of what they see, hear, and *do,* according to a 1988 study reported in *Computers and Personnel.* Multimedia allows the audience to actively participate in the presentation.

Companies in every sector of business have begun to discover that delivering their presentation message through multimedia captivates audiences and illustrates ideas in a way that traditional, written instruction cannot. With visual and auditory reinforcement, people learn and master the information more quickly. The Institute for Defense Analysis showed that multimedia improved students' learning by 15 to 25 percent in their studies.

The Alabama Resource Center (financed primarily by the Alabama Power Co., a public utility with a vested interest in how many electric power consumers come and live in Alabama) is a good example of multimedia in action. The resource center uses multimedia to educate prospective residents on the virtues of Alabama; they can go to one place instead of traveling all over the state. Through a clever multimedia tour, the center can show off the state's highlights.

Has it worked? Yes. The center has helped 30 major companies, such as Mercedes-Benz and Martin-Marietta, with their decisions to relocate to Alabama.

Multimedia can transform the training process as well. For example, Boeing developed a multimedia training course for its new 777 aircraft. In an effort to keep ground time short and mechanics up-to-date on the best procedures for replacing parts, Boeing developed a multimedia training course. When an aircraft arrives with a mechanical problem, the mechanics can tune into a "just-in-time" training program and get specific instruction on the procedures to fix the problem. It sure beats looking through a stack of training manuals.

But for our purposes, the business presentation, multimedia has a special place. It can help communicate project status, provide updates, and reach out to show information that would be impossible with two-dimensional presentation materials.

Persuasive Presentations

Consider the plant manager trying to get a capital budget approved for new equipment. Of course, the manager could bring a stack of numbers, depreciation schedules, and facts to the budget meeting. But now consider an innovative approach. She could add a 60-second video clip to her presentation to show the poor condition of the roof, assembly lines, or other parts of the facility. Chances are, by showing and telling management about the condition of the plant, she'll stand a much better chance of getting her project approved.

I know of one information systems manager who used a similar technique to gain approval to fund a network redesign. She incorporated a few seconds of video and audio clips that showed the poor condition of the network wire closet and then interviewed a few users who complained about the unreliable condition of the network. Especially powerful was one 30-second video clip that showed a salesperson talking about an incident when he lost a day's worth of sales effort because he couldn't get to his information on the network server. He said it may have cost the firm thousands of dollars in lost opportunity. It didn't take long for management to appreciate the problem. It took even less time for them to approve the budget request once they saw—and heard—the problem firsthand.

MULTIMEDIA MYTHS

Like any other new technology, multimedia is surrounded by myths. Naysayers would have you believe it is expensive, difficult, and time-consuming. In fact, none of these concerns needs to be true for today's business presenter. You can control the cost and complexity of multimedia by carefully selecting your tools and keeping your projects within your own competency level.

Most business presenters find that they can master the newer multimedia tools easily. While they are unlikely to create an epic production, business presenters can find tools to make interesting add-in clips for presentations.

It's Expensive

No doubt, your next question is, But isn't this expensive? Yes, getting ready for a multimedia presentation will cost you some money, but you can control costs by cleverly using new tools and stock images.

Thanks to higher sales volume, the cost of equipment necessary for developing and delivering multimedia presentations has fallen fast in the last few years. For example, the necessary hardware to play multimedia material—a sound board and a CD-ROM drive—adds only about $200 to the cost of a new, high-end computer. Specialized software that lets you create multimedia presentations usually costs no more than regular desktop presentation software, sound and art libraries are reasonably priced, and even special gear (like video-image capture boards) costs less than $500.

Of course, if you delve into some of the equipment and software designed for professionals, you can end up spending a lot of money. Some software for professionals costs over $5,000. If you insist on capturing original video, you'll spend a lot of money directing a video crew. For most business presentations, however, you'll be pleased with the quality of reasonably priced hardware and software. And if you learn to add spice to your presentations, your audience will be pleased too.

Another way to save money is to use stock video images. A host of vendors have conveniently placed short video images on CDs and sell them royalty-free for $49 to $99. You can easily buy short video clips of office scenes, business settings, cities, traffic, and any number of other topics. Then, to add these stock video clips to your presentation, you need only cut and paste them into your work.

It's Difficult to Create

Basic multimedia concepts are not difficult to learn. Most of us, however, have never taken a course in video production, so we do have some learning to do. But that doesn't mean we haven't already learned a bit about video concepts. If you consider how many television programs and videos you've seen over the years, you may discover that you've gained a lot of experience in video techniques. Just about every TV show, commercial, and movie you've watched has made an impression on you. By thinking about which shows you liked and which you disliked, you can use your experience to give you a head start in making your own videos.

This chapter provides enough quick tips to get you started. You can also find a number of books dedicated to the finer aspects of creating multimedia at your local bookstore. Even better, look for multimedia training courses that teach the technology through demonstrations or hands-on learning.

It's Time-Consuming

It's true that creating multimedia presentations will take you longer than standard presentations. As a rule of thumb, it takes an expert one hour to produce one minute of video. Novices like me (and probably you, if you're reading this chapter) can expect to spend several hours piecing together a video clip for a presentation.

Keep in mind, however, that a business presentation doesn't have to use a video clip for every single visual. Generally, you can keep your audience tuned in if you include a video clip as you introduce every major topic. Depending on the length of the presentation, you might only have to show two or three video clips.

Further, you'll find that video clips can help make your point faster than any other method. A 15- to 30-second video clip can say as much as 10 minutes of verbal explanation.

WHAT YOU'LL NEED TO GET STARTED

There are differences in the types of equipment you'll need to play back or create multimedia business presentations. You'll use far less computer gear for simply viewing a multimedia presentation than you will to create it. A standard Windows-based multimedia computer can show multimedia presentations fairly well. But to create your own video-enriched multimedia presentations, you'll have to use top-of-the-line hardware.

Playing Multimedia Presentations

To simply view multimedia, you'll need an industry-standard computer with special drivers installed. Using the Windows operating system, you can view most multimedia files by installing Video for Windows. The only special equipment required to play back multimedia presentations is sound capability and sometimes a CD-ROM drive. A high-resolution monitor, a fast processor, and extra memory help make the playback experience even better. The quality of your video playback is influenced by the power the processor uses in your computer. Table 7-1 shows the performance you can expect for various screen sizes. For comparison, keep in mind that television plays at 30 frames per second (fps), but many video presentations are acceptable at half that rate. As you can see, full-screen productions require the fastest processors for best results; but quarter-screen productions might be quite acceptable in a business presentation. This is true especially when your video is meant to relate concepts, not present detailed information.

A special run-time version of the software, which lets you play back (but not create) presentations is sometimes required, depending on who created the software. Many vendors now support the Microsoft and Intel standard .AVI files, which simply require you to install Video for Windows on your computer. If you don't already have that program

Table 7–1 Processor Performance for Video Playback

Processor	Full Screen	¼ Screen	¹⁄₁₆ Screen
486, SX-25	1 fps	15 fps	30 fps
486, DX2-66	10 fps	30 fps	30 fps
Pentium, 60 MHz	20 fps	30 fps	30 fps

installed, you can download a copy from on-line services such as CompuServe or America Online.

For your presentation, you'll also need to check that your projection device can handle multimedia images. Some older, color LCD projection panels cannot handle resolutions above standard VGA. This might make some screen images appear grainy. (It's always a good idea to test out all equipment before your presentation so you don't get a nasty surprise.)

In a large room, you should also make sure you hook up the sound capability to the speaker system so that everyone can hear it. Usually a technician with audiovisual experience can assist you in setting up a large room.

Creating Multimedia Presentations

To create multimedia presentations, you'll need to be a bit more discriminating about equipment. You'll need at least one computer with extra memory, disk space, and peripherals. Although most multimedia equipment that is geared to the business professional works on industry-standard PCs, you should use a high-end computer. If you plan to create multimedia presentations, your computer system should include the following components:

➤ Fast processor (Pentium-class) PC with lots of memory (over 16MB)

➤ Plenty of free space on your hard disk—or, better yet, an additional hard disk reserved only for your media (500MB or more)

➤ High-resolution monitor

➤ 16-bit sound board

➤ Video capture board

➤ Either a mouse or a drawing tablet

➤ Dual- or quad-speed CD-ROM drive

➤ Stereo speakers with volume controls

➤ Microphone

➤ Flat-bed color scanner

➤ VCR with its own monitor

➤ Color printer

Table 7-2 fills in the details of a suggested configuration. Keep in mind that as new hardware and software comes along, you should

Table 7–2 Hardware Recommendations for Creating Multimedia Presentations

Component	Minimum	Recommended
Computer CPU	486 chip, 66 MHz or higher	Pentium chip, 60 MHz or higher
RAM (memory)	16MB	32MB or more
Free hard disk space	500MB	800MB
Video	256-color VGA	16.7-million-color VGA
CD-ROM	Dual speed	Quad speed
Sound board	8-bit	16-bit or higher
Microphone	Standard Windows sound system	Professional quality
Flat-bed scanner	400 dpi or more	24-bit color
VCR with monitor	Any 4-head VCR and TV set	Combo unit (VCR and TV screen) that sits beside your workstation
Printer (black-and-white)	300-dpi laser	600-dpi laser

reevaluate your needs. The more you use multimedia equipment, the more you'll want to get. Luckily, prices continue to decline.

Taking It on the Road

If you are delivering your multimedia presentation on the road, you probably will want to take along a laptop or notebook computer. Be sure to check your computer carefully; don't simply assume that your video and sound files will run.

Several computer makers and other high-tech companies—NEC, IBM, Texas Instruments, Zenith, and Toshiba—pioneered the multimedia notebook market. Competitors enter the market almost monthly. These companies put together lightweight, portable computers especially configured for multimedia presentations with factory integrated sound capability and CD-ROM drives. Generally these computers come with premium price tags well over standard notebook computers. You can expect to pay anywhere from 50 to 80 percent more for a multimedia notebook computer than you would for a standard one. The higher price tag might be worth it, however, saving you from having to add components yourself.

If you are budget-minded, already have a notebook computer you like, or are adventurous, you may wish to add sound and CD-ROM capabilities to your existing notebook or laptop computer. You can usually add sound through an add-on card that fits into the credit card–like slot of your computer (called the PCMCIA slot). New Media Corporation makes a PCMCIA sound card called the Wave Jammer that is among the easiest to install.

You will also need a portable CD-ROM player. The easiest way to put a CD-ROM player on a portable computer is through the parallel (printer) port. MicroSolutions makes a portable unit called the BackPack. It easily attaches to the computer's parallel port and plays CDs at acceptable speeds. Since large videos make extraordinary demands on hardware, it's best to test out how well any given multimedia presentation works. If the video playback looks too slow or jerky on the screen, try reducing the video image to a smaller size.

An Overview of Multimedia Programs

Depending on what you want to do, you have a variety of programs to choose from. If your level of interactivity is low, use a presentation graphics program like PowerPoint or Persuasion. If you need a moderate level of interactivity (buttons, jump to a particular slide), use a program like Freelance Graphics, Action!, or Compel. If you need a high level of control, you'll need a programming authoring tool such as HSC Interactive, ToolBook, or Authorware.

Action!

Start using Action!, from Macromedia, by watching the videotape that comes with it. It gives you an overview of the program and specific guidelines on how to get started.

Action! has three primary tools: Action Tool, which gives movement to an object; Sound Tool, which produces sound over time; and Linking Tool, which causes objects to interact. The program uses a timeline, shown in Figure 7-1, to give a graphical view of the presentation over time; a scene sorter for reordering scenes; and a contents list for editing and changing different elements within scenes.

You can import BMP, EPS, PCX, GIF, TIFF, and PICT graphic file formats into Action! as well, and it supports WAV, MIDI, and CD Audio sound formats. Animation file formats include Macromind Director and FLC/FLI. Video formats supported include Video for Windows, QuickTime for Windows, and QuickTime for Macintosh. Screens may be run on the computer with the player, printed out, or sent to videotape.

Action! comes with a CD-ROM full of animations, clip art, sounds, and ready-to-use templates. You can import presentation files from other formats such as PowerPoint and Persuasion and then add Action!'s multimedia elements to them.

Authorware Professional

Authorware Professional, also from Macromedia, is designed for higher-level interactivity. It uses a visual, icon-based format for creating

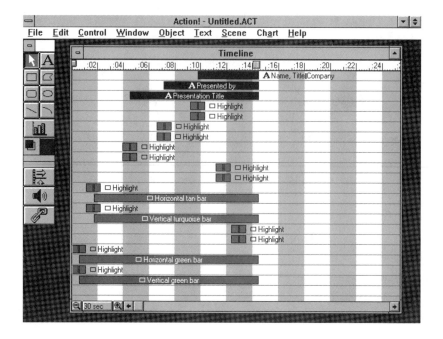

Figure 7-1   Action!'s timeline shows time and layer relationships.

the program flow. Icons represent basic activities such as displaying a screen of information and adding animation or sound.

To build a presentation, you drag an icon and place it on the flowline (Figure 7-2). Double-click on the icon to add attributes to it. To add sound, you simply double-click to bring up the options for loading and playing a sound file. You can add additional attributes such as the number of times a sound plays and at what speed.

Program flow controls, such as branches and loops, are programmed by the Decision and Interaction icons. Interactions can be everything from push-buttons to click/touch (hotspot) areas. A click-touch area is an area on the screen that a user can activate by clicking, double-clicking, or moving the cursor over the hotspot.

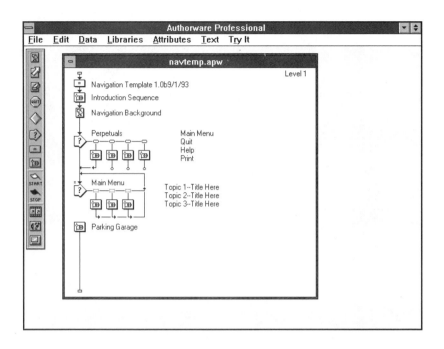

Figure 7–2　It's easy to build a flowing presentation with Authorware Professional.

The Calculation icon performs math and logical functions, and handles a wide range of variables. You group any series of icons together into a Map icon, which forces the program into smaller, manageable chunks.

Authorware Professional is a complex program that may take some time to master. It comes with a tutorial, good documentation, sample applications, and sample models.

HSC Interactive

HSC Interactive, from HSC Software, is an icon-based Windows package that is actually a subset of AimTech's IconAuthor, only with fewer icons. You'll get a package high on multimedia content but low on interaction.

In HSC Interactive, you take icons from a scroll bar and place them on a visual flowchart. You define the attributes for the icons through settings in dialog boxes and content windows.

It includes a graphics editor to create graphics files and an animation program to animate graphic files. It also has a screen capture and resolution editor.

Compel

Compel, from Asymetrix, looks like a presentation program—it has an outliner, slide sorter, and graphic tools—but it also adds an interactivity feature. You can link any object on a slide to another slide, and an object can trigger an event. Compel comes with a CD-ROM full of clip art.

ToolBook

Multimedia ToolBook for Windows, from Asymetrix, has been described as "HyperCard for Windows" (a reference to HyperCard, Apple Computer's information management tool for the Macintosh). It combines a scripting language with visual tools. ToolBook is a popular format for producing *hypermedia* applications under Windows. In a hypermedia application, readers move through the information as they wish, jumping from key word to key word rather than page to page in a strict, defined sequence.

Using its "hotword" feature, you can assign a script to a word or phrase in a page of text. This feature makes it easy to create pop-up explanations or page jumps. You can also create "hotword graphics" by including graphics in your hotwords.

ToolBook organizes applications into books with pages that represent the application's screen. You view the pages in windows called "viewers." ToolBook comes with many sample scripts and complete applications to help newcomers learn by example.

Popular applications for ToolBook include hypertext books, database programs, and tutorials. *NautilusCD,* a CD-ROM publication from Metatec, is based on the ToolBook engine.

Astound

Astound, from Gold Disk, which runs on both Macintosh and PC platforms, lets you play Macintosh-created files in Windows. It also has an outliner and charting, interactivity, and animation features. You can import PowerPoint and Freelance Graphic presentations directly.

Astound creates your multimedia presentation by associating each component or object of the presentation with a timeline, as shown in Figure 7-3. This timeline lets you specify how long it will take for an object to enter and exit the screen and how long it will be displayed. You can then synchronize a narration with words moving across the screen. You can also use any picture in a pictograph (a columnar chart that uses stacks of pictures instead of plain bars to represent data).

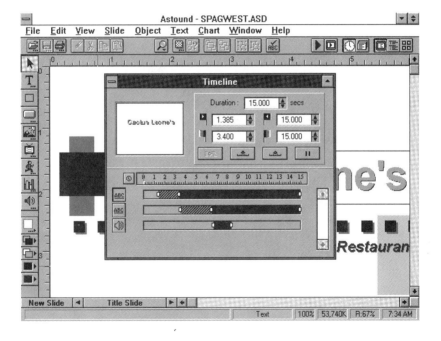

Figure 7–3 Astound's Timeline window controls the sequence and timing of events.

You control all aspects of the presentation from user-definable buttons, responses, and transition effects. The CD-ROM for the PC contains over 1,000 clip sounds, images, and video; the Macintosh version also contains sample files, sounds and images but does not include a CD-ROM.

A QUICK COURSE: CREATING THE SHOW

Multimedia support for your business presentations will often consist of putting together video and still images, sound effects, and transitions between scenes. In this section I'll talk about each of the components of a typical business presentation.

Sound

Most multimedia software lets you add musical tracks, special sound effects, and voice-overs easily. Although you may want to use them all, do so sparingly. If you create a short video clip (15 to 30 seconds) to enhance your general presentation, it helps to add appropriate sound effects.

Consider using upbeat music as a background to your video clip. You can usually find libraries of music on the same CDs that come with video scenes. Listen and pick out a few favorites.

Also, don't feel that you must use words throughout the video. In fact, sometimes using fewer words is better. Let your video scenes convey your message. Use spoken words simply to enhance or emphasize a point. As an alternative to spoken words, consider using single words or short bullet points as text that overlays your video scenes. This effect helps convey your message to the audience and adds variety to your presentation.

Video

Video adds a lot of support to a presentation. You don't have to use it for every occasion, but it might help you make your point. If you are in doubt, try putting together a clip for an upcoming presentation. If you work for a large company, you might be able to borrow someone else's equipment. Alternatively, you can call office supply stores or copy shops to see if they will rent you time on their video editing computers.

According to Ron Wodaski, author of the brilliant book *Multimedia Madness!* (Sams), there are five key areas to producing a video: moving images, transitions, content, timing, and pace. These key areas are the nuts and bolts of putting together quick video clips that work in business presentations. The following sections give you some special tips and tricks for each of the areas that Wodaski defined.

Moving Images

Use movement, not static images, in your multimedia clips. You want to have images that jump out and dazzle the audience. If you on occasion do have to use still pictures, be careful to change them in and out rapidly. Your audience shouldn't see a still image for more than five or seven seconds.

When you film people talking, avoid "talking head" shots. Place your subject in an interesting setting, such as in a park, on the beach, or along a corridor in the office. There are two benefits to this approach: It will make the scene more interesting and the speaker will probably be more relaxed. It will be much easier for the speaker to look and act candid if he or she is not stuck behind a desk or hemmed into a two-square-foot area of a stage.

Remember that too much of a good thing is still too much. Allow for the audience to take an occasional pause with a still (or slow-moving) image. If possible, coordinate the transition from movement to still image with the beats of background music.

Transitions

Since most videos and multimedia presentations consist of a series of clips connected together, you'll want to use transitions as a way to move from one scene to another. There are six basic types of transitions: wipes, splits, spots, blinds, boxes, and dissolves. Depending on the video editing software you use, you may have a considerable selection of transitions.

It helps to plan your transitions so you don't make too much of a statement. For most uses, wipes, splits, and spots are good transitions to introduce a new subject, while blinds, boxes, and dissolves help connect same-subject segments. And watch your timing. When transitioning to a new scene relating to the same subject, use longer durations. A one- to two-second transition is usually appropriate. When introducing a new subject, make it snappier. Make it a half- to one-and-a-half–second transition.

Figure 7-4 shows the six basic types of transitions, which are each described briefly in the following sections.

Wipes These give the audience an immediate sense of change; they change one scene to another by covering up the scene abruptly. Wipes can go from left to right, right to left, top to bottom, or bottom to top, or it can even move diagonally. Wipes occur quickly and break into the new scene within a half to one-and-a-half seconds. Some software packages offer a "clock wipe," which wipes in a clockwise motion. Use this effect when you want to convey the notion of time passing.

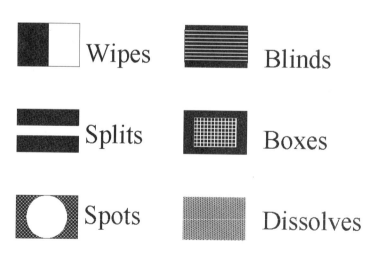

Figure 7–4   Examples of transitions

Splits Like wipes, splits create a mood that something very different is in store for the audience. They are good for new-subject transitions. You can use a split from the center of the screen to cut open to the new scene either vertically or horizontally. Sometimes you can use a different color to emphasize the change. Splits should move briskly and break into the new scene within a half to one-and-a-half seconds.

Spots These are also akin to wipes. Generally they start in the center of the screen, then opens to the new scene as a round iris, square, or diamond shape. It produces a dramatic effect appropriate for introducing new subjects.

Blinds These open the new scene with small vertical or horizontal bars. It is an effective, new-subject transition that can also be used for dramatic same-subject changes. Depending on your software, you can choose the number and thickness of the blinds. The thicker the blind, the more dramatic the effect.

Boxes You can use random boxes to create a transition from one scene to another, either to introduce a new subject or to change the scene within the same subject area. Most software lets you either adjust the size of the boxes or how the boxes change—vertically or horizontally. Avoid overusing boxes, because they will become too noticeable and distract your subject.

Dissolves Fading the picture from one video scene to another is a very effective same-subject transition. You may choose to fade to a color first, such as red or black, then to the new scene, or fade one scene into another.

Some video editors like to use a technique called "morphing" to metamorphose or change one image into another. This is very effective to show continuity. You'll need special software to create the morphing effect.

Content

Vary the content from people to images throughout your production. Make sure people don't look too stilted when they appear on the screen. As noted earlier, it helps to tape people in natural settings or walking around, rather than show them behind a desk or podium. You can also create professional and dramatic effects by coming in for a close-up after showing a subject from a distance.

Timing

Video professionals develop a sense of timing when they create a production. Most professionals like to start and end a scene with a lot of action. Since your video editing software can clip a scene wherever you want, you'll have a lot of flexibility here.

You can learn how to count the action beats of a video. A "beat" is any kind of action—moving an object, picking up a pen, or gesturing to the audience. Try to end a clip on a strong beat.

Three-beat clips are considered ideal. If you cannot get the three beats to occur in one clip, consider combining them from different clips.

Pace

When in doubt, keep your clips short. You can bore an audience if your video plods from one subject to another. It's best to keep scenes brief and make your points quickly. Avoid using too many clips that say the same thing unless you are really trying to drive a point home.

Also, don't try to be *too* creative. Just because you bought a multimedia library with 200 exotic video clips, it doesn't mean you should launch a space shuttle in the middle of your scene of a stockholders' meeting!

Finally, even though you will want to move along quickly, don't move things so fast that your audience doesn't understand your message. As you build your presentation, it's a good idea to get a second opinion on your pacing.

MOVING ON

While this chapter presented some of the basics, I encourage you to read other books and magazine articles on creating and using multimedia. New periodicals about the topic are springing up all the time. Check your newsstand.

In Part III, I discuss techniques on presenting: how-to's and tips on training your voice, finding your best standing position, and special considerations for speaking on television or radio.

PRESENTING

In this part, I turn your attention to the special style and techniques that you'll need to deliver a polished presentation. I focus on helping you develop your own personal style, increase your effectiveness, and make your point. I also discuss setting up your room and the different room layouts that you may encounter. Finally, I discuss presenting with electronic media and the special considerations you'll need for making electronic presentations. As you'll soon see, it's true to some extent that "it's not *what* you say, but *how* you say it."

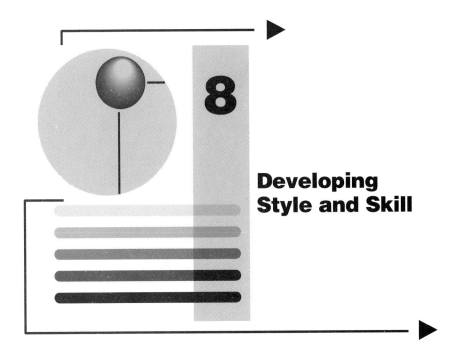

Developing Style and Skill

There is no magic to making a good speech. You do not have to be a born speaker. Just as the proper techniques for swinging a golf club effectively can be analyzed, understood, practiced, and applied, so too can the techniques for becoming an effective speaker. You don't have to be a natural at presentations, but you do have to pay attention to the details and the elements of making a good speech.

In this chapter, I explore the basics of speechmaking. I look at some simple techniques that, if practiced (and practiced, and practiced), will improve your chances of *making your point*. I explore the basics of speech making and counter the #1 objection to speaking before a group: fear. Then I take a look at basic techniques like developing "presenter's posture" and learning how to work with your voice. No doubt you'll learn a few new techniques to try out on your next business presentation.

LEARNING TO BE A NATURAL AT PUBLIC SPEAKING

Good speakers are trained, not born. While there are many people who deliver business presentations, there aren't a lot of dynamic speakers. Experience and practice alone won't transform you into a good speaker. I know of one senior executive of a large Fortune 100 company who gave speeches weekly for over 20 years. His presentations were horrible—dry and boring. He mumbled his words and never altered the pitch or tone of his voice. Experience didn't make him any better.

Conversely, practicing along with constructive coaching can make a wonderful difference. It can turn an average speaker into a very dynamic one. Take, for example, Microsoft's famous chairman, Bill Gates. Years ago Gates was dubbed "Boring" Gates by many who emerged from his speeches. His talks were monotonous and drab, and he often stood in a "fig-leaf" stance. Despite the fact that he had a great message to deliver, lots of it got lost in the boredom.

At some point in the late '80s, Gates was called upon to deliver a major industry keynote address. He was to introduce his new vision of computing. But this time, he did something different. He worked with a speech coach and effectively changed his speaking style. I saw Gates before and after the transformation. The difference was incredible. Within less than a six-week period, his style was transformed. He spoke clearly, didn't mumble, paused effectively, and stood comfortably and with good posture. He had a great message, as before, but this time people *heard* it. From that point on, Gates has become an entertaining and informative speaker. People crowd convention centers and stand in long lines at trade shows just to hear him speak. Most people who see him now would never guess how bad a speaker he once was.

So if your presentation skills need work, read on for tips based on our observations and experiences. You need to analyze the techniques for good presentations, and then use the ones that fit your personality. Pick a style that feels good for you. Comfort is the key.

CONQUERING FEAR

Zero hour approaches. Soon it will be time to make your point. Your outline is well developed, you've done the research, and your visuals are clear, crisp, and colorful. Time to rest and relax, right?

Probably not. Most business presenters, especially new ones, find themselves anything but relaxed before the big day. If you feel a little queasy or find your stomach in knots, don't despair. Everyone, even the seasoned professional, goes through a little anxiety before a presentation.

As mentioned in Chapter 1, survey after survey points out that the fear of public speaking ranks at the top of the list of things that people dread. Because speaking brings such intense nervousness, it causes many people to worry about doing embarrassing things. They worry about spilling their coffee, stumbling up the steps to the podium, forgetting their notes, and a whole host of other mishaps.

I have a speech to give!

No doubt you've heard the horror stories. There's the one about the accountant who was asked to speak at an industry conference. Once on stage, she found herself having difficulty forming her words. Her mouth went dry, her knees knocked, and she could hardly complete two sentences without a stammer. Somehow, having managed to complete her talk, her fingers clasped around the lectern so tightly that she was unable to relax her grip. Only as the lectern hit the ground did she manage to let go.

Fear plagues most new business presenters. Luckily, with a little work, the anxiety can be turned into a positive force.

Harry Caray, arguably the greatest of all radio baseball announcers, said that sometimes it is very difficult to find that feeling. During his years in St. Louis as the voice of the Cardinals, he told a banquet audience what "butterflies" meant to him. He said that on those days when he awoke with his tummy churning just a bit in nervous anticipation, he knew he would be alert, creative, colorful, and at his best.

On those days when he didn't have any butterflies, he feared he would not be at his best. He spoke of sitting alone somewhere in the ballpark and working on himself to "fire up." He would try to stimulate himself with fear by repeating over and over "there are millions of people who will be listening to every word you say. Don't screw it up."

Anyone who has listened to Harry Caray has heard something special. Besides his trademark "Hooooooly Coooooow!" and singing of "Take Me Out to the Ballgame" during the seventh inning stretch of each Cubs home game, he has told us what was happening on the field *when* it was happening. You could see what was happening on the field in your mind's eye through his words, his feelings, his enunciation, his pace, and his excitement.

Unlike some play-by-play announcers, Harry did not watch a play and then tell you what happened. He described the play as it was happening. To do that day in and day out, play after play, he had to be ready, alert, and on top of his art. When he felt the butterflies prior to the start of a game, he knew he would be able to do his best.

Fight or Flight

Adrenaline = Energy

The shelves of your local bookstore are probably filled with volumes that address techniques for stress reduction. The techniques most frequently cited—learning how to breathe, stretching and relaxation exercises, concentrating and tuning out extraneous thoughts—also work for overcoming the fear of giving a business presentation.

Professional speech coaches advise their clients to take the anxiety and fear of speaking and turn it into energy. When people are physically confronted, their glands release adrenaline, activating the body for a "fight or flight" response. The hormone increases blood pressure and raises the heartbeat. In short, it causes a physical reaction, and that reaction can be converted to energy.

The Mental Checklist

The best way for dealing with the surge of adrenaline before a speech is to work through a mental exercise that confirms that everything is in order. For example, you should be confident in the following eight items:

➤ My presentation is set up—in the computer, on the slide projector, etc.

➤ My speaker notes are in place.

➤ I know my opening statement.

➤ I plan to make the following point(s).

➤ I know how I will handle questions during the presentation.

➤ My extra backup or resource material is at hand.

➤ I will make the following point(s) as a closing remark.

➤ I will (or won't) stay to answer questions after my prepared comments.

Going through this mental checklist should reassure you that your are prepared for your presentation. If you've been able to confirm each point, it is unlikely that you'll make any structural faux pas because you forgot something.

Next, you should find a few minutes to be by yourself. Steal away to your office and close the door. Take a few deep breaths and practice some relaxation exercises. Start at the top of your head and work down, tensing your muscles and then letting go. Move your head from side to side, do a few shoulder rolls, and stretch your arms up, down, and around. Keep breathing deeply.

It's amazing the physical effect you'll get by doing a few of these exercises and taking in some extra air. Deep breathing is among the best techniques for getting fear under control.

Last-Minute Adjustments

In the moments before you begin your presentation, your focus and concentration should be on not falling down as you walk onto the stage— I'm serious! What are the physical obstacles between where you are standing or sitting now and where you will be presenting? Look for them now. You should have looked for them during your practice session, but some new obstacle may have arisen since then, such as an extension cord or an additional chair. Look for those changes and plan your path.

Check your clothes. Is anything showing that shouldn't be? If you are wearing a button-down shirt, check that your shirt collar is indeed buttoned down.

Take one last look at yourself in a mirror. If you are wearing makeup, has it smeared or do you need to reapply the lipstick? If you're wearing a tie, is the knot dead-center perfect?

If you are wearing a suit, button your suit coat. Reach both hands behind you, grab the bottom of your suit coat, and pull it down. This will get your coat lying properly over your shoulders. (It's embarrassing to walk out with the back of your coat pulled up above your belt, and the front of the coat beginning to cover your knees.)

Check all of your zippers! An unchecked, unsecured zipper can cause the most embarrassing moment of all and a humiliating moment that will be remembered for life.

All of this last-minute double-checking serves several purposes:

- ▶ You only have one chance to make a positive first impression. Looking your best when you first appear helps you win over the audience.
- ▶ Adjusting everything beforehand means you won't have to fidget on stage.
- ▶ Each and every adjustment you make escalates your confidence level.
- ▶ You won't fall down as you walk to center stage.

Last-Minute No-No

As you walk to the front of the room, you may begin to feel that the opening of your presentation is really weak. Resist the temptation to walk up and ad lib your way through something you have not practiced. If your preparation was as it should have been, trust yourself and use the opening that you prepared. Do not doubt yourself or your material now!

SPEAKING TIPS AND TECHNIQUES

Good business presenters develop their skills by working on basic techniques. These can be as simple as learning how to stand, breathe, speak, and relax.

The following sections cover simple techniques that should help you feel more comfortable during your next presentation.

Finding Your Personal Style

One good way to discover your personal style for presentations is by trying out several different styles in a videotaped practice session. Make exaggerated facial expressions or tell a joke or anecdote. Pretend the lens of the camera is a member of your audience and spend a little time speaking directly to the camera. (I know this seems difficult, but if you can convince the camera, you can probably convince your boss.) Speak fast, speak slow, and alter the tone of your voice. Tell a story, pause, and pick up again. Try out different gestures with your hands. Don't forget to smile once in a while.

When you are finished, watch your video immediately. Instant feedback will help you correct any problems. It will also give you a chance to confirm or change your style. You be the judge. Find the presentation style that you like best. Then get back in front of the camera and go through your speech again. This time, spend most of the time reinforcing the style that you liked.

Standing Tall

New business presenters often make the same mistakes. They don't know how to stand and they don't know what to do with their hands.

Learn how to create a balanced stance. Start by standing straight up, with your back to the wall. Now click your heels back to the wall and force your legs back to try to touch the wall. Then pull your shoulders and head up. Align them to touch the wall. Finally, try to force the small of your back into the wall too. Uncomfortable? Probably, but you are also standing very erect.

Too Comfortable & Just Right

Next, take two steps away from the wall, trying not to alter your posture too much. Place your feet about 10 to 12 inches apart. Distribute your weight equally. Then relax your knees by bending them slightly. Relax your shoulders if they feel too tight, but continue to keep your head and chin up.

At this point you should be standing very erect, but comfortably. That's the balanced stance. You are in a perfect speaking position. You don't have your weight shifted on one side or another, your chest is up, and you can breathe deeply. Your hands and arms are relaxed and down at your sides, not bent in any way.

If you were to look at yourself in the mirror, you might be surprised to see how comfortable and confident you appear. Learning and maintaining a good posture for speaking brings several benefits. First, you'll look and feel in command of yourself and the situation. Second, you won't distract your audience by shifting from side to side. Third, you'll improve the tonal quality of your voice because you are standing tall, breathing well, and can speak from down in your diaphragm.

Cultivating a Speaker's Voice

Most business presenters never took voice lessons. Chances are you were never given training about how and when to alter the tone or pitch of your voice. Yet research shows that over 80 percent of your emotional impact and believability comes from what people hear, not what they see. Use your voice to help deliver the message.

Turn on your video again. Play back what you recorded earlier, only this time close your eyes and just listen. What do you hear? Is it convincing? Does it sound sincere? Is it monotonous? How about your timing?

Effective business presenters learn how to use their voices to project the message. They enunciate words clearly and speak with rhythm. Frequently, good presenters learn how to interject silence into the speech. Silence or an effective pause gives the audience a chance to digest a comment. This can be powerful when you are introducing new ideas.

If you've never worked with a voice coach, try a few more exercises. Using a tape recorder and a newspaper, read the headline stories, pretending that you are the local newscaster. Alter your voice pitch up and down. Use inflection on key words to give them special emphasis. Now listen to the recording. Sound good? If you used these techniques, it probably does.

Next, try to script out a little of your business presentation. A few paragraphs will probably be enough. Now mark your script. Underline the words you want to emphasize. Use a down arrow to show downward inflection on a word. This is usually done on the last word of a sentence or phrase to give it authority. This will make you sound confident, persuasive, and in command. Use upward inflection of your voice if you want to question or show politeness.

Using Transition Words

Some people develop the habit of saying "ah" or "um" between thoughts and sentences. If you have this tendency, try to overcome it by using transition phrases or pausing between thoughts. Watch your video and note each time you said "ah" or "um"; see if you can't find a good transition term or word to insert at that point in your talk.

Try replacing your filler words with terms like "for example…" or "that takes us to…" or "which means…" Each situation might call for a different expression, but if you study when and how you use "ah," you will be able to eliminate most occurrences.

Giving Yourself a Pep Talk

Have you ever had a conversation with yourself? Lots of people feel better when they give themselves a pep talk before their presentation. It could go something like this:

> *Cheryl, you know what you are talking about; you have what it takes to give this group a great presentation. Nobody knows more about the subject than you. You've done your homework, and you know this information is going to be good for them. Besides, this is exciting stuff; you are going to tell them something really important.*

Self-delivered pep talks can really help. If you honestly believe that you are about to give a good presentation, chances are you'll make it a self-fulfilling prophesy.

Relaxing through Deep Breathing

As I mentioned earlier in this chapter, you can help your presentation style by learning how to relax. A few breathing exercises can really help.

Before any presentation, try to get a few minutes to yourself. Practice deep breathing. Stand straight, lean forward slightly, take in as much air as you can through your nose, relax your stomach muscles, and extend your stomach as if you were trying to fill it with air. Hold it for five or ten counts, then blow out the air through your mouth. Repeat the process a couple of times (not too quickly or you'll get dizzy).

Deep breathing exercises can be the presenter's easiest and best tool for stress reduction. You should also try to take a few minutes to tense up and relax your major muscles before going on stage.

Pre-speech Checklist

Finally, here's a list of details that will help you put yourself and your style in order. (Make sure you can answer yes to these details.)

Material

- ❑ You know the material.
- ❑ You put this presentation together from start to finish.
- ❑ You are an expert on the subject matter.
- ❑ No one in the audience knows your subject better than you do.
- ❑ You are confident of your research.

Presentation Skills

- ❑ You can enunciate your words clearly.
- ❑ You have chosen your words carefully.
- ❑ You don't ramble.
- ❑ You have prepared good examples, analogies, or anecdotes.
- ❑ You are comfortable with your pace.
- ❑ You know your timing. Remember, a presentation is not a race against the clock.

Appearance

- ❑ Your clothing is pressed and professional-looking.
- ❑ You've taken time to select your apparel. (Spend a few extra minutes to ensure that the colors blend. Will this outfit be appropriate to the occasion?) We all have a favorite business suit or dress. If you feel that your favorite will be appropriate, wear it. Wearing an outfit you really feel good in contributes to a positive attitude.

❑ You feel well groomed. Look at yourself in the mirror several days before the presentation and ask yourself if the length of your hair is appropriate. Hair style and color is important. Make sure that when you are presenting there will not be any nagging thoughts that make you wish you had been to the hairdresser.

❑ Do your accessories blend with your outfit, hair color, eyeliner, and other makeup colors? You never know what the audience may discover in your appearance that will distract them. Watch out for wild colors in front of a conservative business group. As a general rule, wild colors such as burnt orange, any shade of red, and bright or iridescent colors are not appropriate. These colors distract. Go with subtle, quiet colors so the audience will be attracted to your face, not to a brightly colored accessory you're wearing.

❑ Look in the mirror, but mentally put yourself into the audience. What do you see? If you were seeing this person for the first time, what would you think? Would you trust or respect the person that you see?

Practice Makes Perfect

❑ You have practiced the entire presentation more times than you care to remember; you can say it backwards and forwards and in your sleep.

❑ You have practiced speaking from your script or notes and you are comfortable with these presentation mechanics.

❑ You have practiced when to look at your script or notes and when to look at your audience.

❑ You have practiced with your eyes; you know how to pick out a face in the audience and speak to that face for a minimum of three seconds.

❑ You have practiced how to move your eyes to another face, focus on it, and speak to it.

❏ If you are using presentation software, you have practiced looking only at the screen on your computer, not the screen behind you.

❏ You have practiced what to do with pages of your script or notes when you no longer need them; you know where you are going to put those pages, and you know how to put them there as you finish with each one.

❏ You have practiced where to put your hands and how to use them if you are working from behind a podium.

❏ You have practiced how to use your hands if you are not using a podium and are totally exposed to the audience.

❏ You have practiced your posture—upright but not stiff, presenting a comfortable appearance.

❏ You have practiced with the equipment you are using; you are comfortable using it during your presentation.

❏ If you are going to move from the podium, you know where you are going to go, how long it will take you to get there, how long you will remain there, and how long it will take you to return. You have also taken the time to study the floor, making yourself aware of anything that might cause a stumble. Finally, you have practiced a comfortable return to the podium to ensure that there are no gaps in your presentation.

❏ You have practiced how to use a podium microphone.

❏ You have practiced how to use *this* podium microphone.

❏ You know not to speak directly into the microphone because you can "pop" the microphone with any "p-words," and you know how distracting that is to an audience.

❏ You know how to talk over the top of the podium microphone.

❏ You know how to always talk to the podium microphone. It stays in one place. You cannot move away from it. You gather in the audience primarily through the use of your eyes, not the movement of your head.

❑ You have practiced using a lavaliere microphone, one that is clipped to your necktie or lapel. You know that you have more freedom of movement with this type of microphone; as your body turns, the "lav" turns with you.

❑ You have practiced with a hand-held wireless microphone, and you know how to talk over it and not into it.

❑ You have practiced moving the handheld, wireless microphone with the turn of your head to ensure that the audience hears a consistent level of sound.

❑ At the conclusion, you have practiced how to thank the audience and exit the stage.

❑ If you are using a lavaliere microphone that is not wireless, you have practiced taking it off and placing it somewhere before you walk from the stage. (There is nothing more embarrassing than thanking the audience, beginning to exit the stage, and having the lavaliere ripped from your tie as the cord becomes taut and bangs down on the floor.)

Now that you are totally comfortable with your presentation skills, you'll want to make sure that the room and setup is the way you want it for best results. I discuss this in the next chapter.

9

Setting up
the Room

Poor Joe Andersen. He was all ready to deliver his business presentation. He'd prepared for weeks, knew his material, and committed nearly every visual to memory. He practiced his presentation in front of a video, fine-tuned it, and practiced again. But twenty minutes before the presentation, he got a call. The meeting had been moved to the executive conference room. Joe had never set foot inside that room. He didn't know what kind of audiovisual equipment it had—or even how to turn on the lights. He panicked.

Luckily, he found an administrative assistant who showed him around. He quickly reloaded his presentation on a laptop computer and headed for the conference room. The assistant gave him a three-minute overview of the room and showed him where to find the light switches, water dispenser, and pens for the white board. Together they rearranged the chairs and made sure everyone would have a good view of the screen. He set up the computer, plugged it into an LCD panel, and turned it on. He adjusted the blinds in the room so the image on the screen was sharp.

It worked. With two minutes to spare, he was all set up in the new room and starting to regain his composure. Whew!

For most business presentations, you'll be luckier than Joe was. You'll have plenty of notice about your room setting and you'll deliver the presentation in familiar surroundings. You'll know every nook and cranny, the layout of your room and where to find the light switches, well in advance. If you need to make special arrangements for bringing in a computer, an easel, or other material, you'll have time to do so.

Whether you deliver your presentation in the conference room down the hall or in a coliseum across the continent, you should plan any adjustments you'll need based on the setting. You should know the room size, setup, lighting, and any special requirements.

In this chapter, I present the room setup options for making your business presentations. For the most part, you'll find yourself in familiar surroundings. But for those occasions where you are called into a new environment, I'll give you tips for making sure everything is in place.

LIGHTS, SOUND, ACTION!

There are only a few rules for setting up a room. First, get into the room well in advance of the presentation. Ideally, set up the day (or night) before. When this isn't practical, show up at least an hour before the presentation (or several hours beforehand, if it is to be a big production in a big room).

Next, check out the lighting and sound. Determine whether you have any control over the lights. For the most part, when you use electronic visuals, such as a computer and projection device, you will need to dim the lights in the front of the room so your audience can see the visuals better. Be careful, however, that you don't dim the room so much that your audience can't see you. You may need to position yourself underneath a light or get a spotlight installed. Also, check out the sound capabilities of the room. Make sure your audience can hear you.

Finally, don't do it all by yourself. Get help. The bigger your audience, the more people you'll need to enlist on your team. Divide and conquer tasks for getting everything set up. Ultimately you, as the presenter, will soar or sink with the presentation, its content, its delivery, and its environment. Try to check and double-check as many of the arrangements as you can personally, but don't try to do everything yourself.

THE FIVE BASIC ROOM FORMATS

Despite the countless variations possible, there are only about five basic types of rooms for most business presentations. They accommodate presentations that range from very small to very large groups. You should review the room, the size of the audience expected, and the special considerations for your presentation. Make sure this planning is done in advance. As a general rule of thumb, the larger the audience, the more planning you need to do.

Conference Room with Table

The easiest room to set up is the classic conference room. For the most part, conference rooms are used for groups of fewer than 12 people. They require a less formal format and are more conducive to discussion during the presentation. Usually chairs are set around the conference table, and the audience sits toward one end of the table while the presenter stands at the head of the table.

Some general guidelines:

▶ If possible, angle the chairs in a U or V format. Your audience will be more comfortable if they can keep their chairs at a right angle with the table, rather than their heads.

▶ Make sure to prearrange any audiovisual equipment you need for the conference room. Don't darken the room too much; most attendees prefer some lighting so they can take notes.

▶ If you are using computer projection equipment, check out the lighting of the room to determine your options. If you must dim the lights so that the visuals are clearly visible, try to dim them just in the front of the room. If you cannot make adjustments with a wall switch, check to see if you can remove the light bulbs in the front of the room.

▶ For a small group, consider using a large-screen monitor or a TV set instead of a projector. At a minimum you'll need a 17-inch screen size, but you'll probably be happier with a 25-inch screen. Make sure you pre-test your presentation in the room. Often different projection devices change the colors of your visuals.

▶ If your presentation requires manual input, check to see whether the room is equipped with a flip chart or whiteboard. If neither is available, you can try to take notes on the computer by opening up another session using a word processor or a blank presentation on your presentation software.

▶ In most cases, you will not need to use a microphone for a conference room presentation. If you are using a multimedia presentation, however, you will need to bring in speakers so your audience can hear the audio portion.

Meeting Room with Tables

Another popular format for business presentations is a meeting room set up with long, narrow tables (see Figure 9-1). The tables give members of your audience a place to take notes, classroom style. Meeting rooms can be set for as few as 12 or as many as 300. Generally, the larger the room, the more formal your format should be.

Some general guidelines:

▶ Usually tables are set for four to six people, with one or two aisles in the middle. Make sure there is ample room for people to get up and move around during breaks.

▶ After you have set up your visuals, take a seat in the very last row and make sure they are legible from that distance.

▶ If the presentation is expected to last over an hour, you should arrange to have pitchers of water and glasses set at each table. Usually one water pitcher for every four people is adequate.

Meeting Room with Tables
Setup for 24 participants (4 to table)

Stage

Table w/pitcher		Table w/pitcher		Table w/pitcher
Table w/pitcher		Table w/pitcher		Table w/pitcher

Figure 9–1   Tables give members of your audience a place to take notes. They may take up precious room but the people will feel more relaxed—a blessing during a day-long seminar.

Make sure the pitcher is set in the middle so that people can reach for it comfortably. You don't want people in the audience having to stand up to reach for water!

▶ If the room is small to mid-sized—set for 40 or fewer people—the audiovisual requirements won't differ from those of a conference room. If you are using computer projection equipment, check out the lighting of the room to determine your options. Since most attendees prefer some lighting so they can take notes, you'll want to adjust the lights carefully; don't make it so dark that the audience can't see you.

▶ If your presentation requires manual input of comments, check to see whether the room is equipped with a flip chart or a whiteboard. But keep in mind that these visuals will be hard to see if you have more than 20 to 25 people in the audience.

▶ If your room is set for more than 40 people, you will probably need a microphone. If you are giving a multimedia presentation, you will need to bring in speakers and hook them up to the room's audio system.

▶ If your room is set for more than 60 people, you should use a stage, riser, or platform so that the people in the back of your audience can see you. If the stage is set away from the computer or projector, try to get a wireless remote device so you can control the visuals. You might also opt to have a podium or presenter's table in the front of the room. In either case, you should have a comfortable place to put your speaker notes.

▶ For an audience of 40 to 60, you should use an LCD panel and projector so that everyone in the audience can see your presentation.

Meeting Room without Tables

You can fit many more people into a meeting room if there are no tables (see Figure 9-2). Watch out for the comfort of your audience, however. Sometimes meeting planners cram too many people into a small space.

Some general guidelines:

▶ Follow the general directions given for a meeting room with tables, except for lighting requirements. You can dim the room lighting more in this situation, because your audience is unlikely to take full notes if they have no place to write but on their laps. Also, try to avoid service items in the room, such as water or other beverages in this setting. It's too easy for someone to trip over a misplaced coffee cup.

▶ If your room is set for more than 40 people, check to see whether you'll need to use a microphone. For more than 60 people, you should use a stage, riser, or platform so that those in the back of your audience can see you. If the stage is set away from the computer or projector, try to get a wireless remote device so you can control the visuals. Alternatively, you could have a podium or presenter's table in the front of the room.

Meeting Room w/o Tables

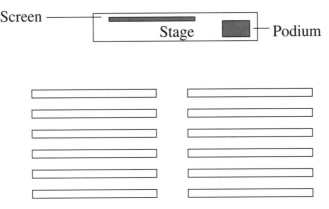

Figure 9–2 Omitting tables allows you to include many more people in a room. Just make sure people don't feel too cramped to enjoy themselves—and the seminar doesn't last too long.

► For an audience of 40 to 60, you should use an LCD panel and projector so everyone in the audience can see your presentation.

Auditorium

Giving a presentation in an auditorium isn't much different from giving one in a meeting room without tables—except that the room is larger and usually better equipped. If you make your presentation in an auditorium, you will probably have to work with a microphone, speakers, special lighting, and a stage.

Some general guidelines:

► Allow yourself a little extra time to get comfortable with the stage and the settings. If you plan on walking around the stage during the presentation (a highly recommended technique), consider marking off stopping points with a piece of masking tape. That way, you'll have a visual cue and keep yourself from walking off the stage if you get carried away with your thoughts.

▶ If the stage is set up with a podium, use it as a place to put your notes; don't hide behind it. Get out to the side of the podium and walk around the stage. Be careful, however, not to plant yourself in front of a visual. You don't want to block anyone's view.

▶ Make sure you get the lighting technician to show you how the lights will look, and make changes if necessary. A hot spotlight shining in your eyes can throw off your timing when you deliver your presentation. Likewise, a misdirected light that misses your face but illuminates the rest of your body is unflattering. (I know, I have a video of one such presentation that I made.)

Banquet Room

Making a business presentation in a banquet room (see Figure 9-3) is an especially challenging experience, during or after a meal. You'll not only have to deal with less-than-ideal lighting, but you'll have to compete with clanking cups and people moving around the room during your presentation.

Some general guidelines:

▶ Walk around the room before the meal is served. Check to see whether there are any poles or other viewing obstructions. Try to get the tables moved if there are problem spots.

▶ If you can control the agenda, try to hold off delivery of your presentation until after dessert is served. You'll avoid much of the distraction that way.

▶ As for room setup, chances are good that people will be seated at multiple round tables. You won't be able to change the seating arrangement very much, but you can ask for help in making yourself more visible. If possible, use a small riser or stage, a microphone, and perhaps a podium.

Banquet Room Setup

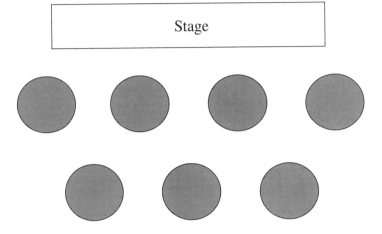

Figure 9–3 Banquet rooms use round tables to seat people more comfortably than at rectangular tables.

- ▶ Use a microphone if you have a group of 20 or more. You'll have a hard-enough time competing with clanking cups.

- ▶ If you use visuals, make sure they are focused very close to you or directly behind you. You'll avoid introducing more distractions and help keep the audience's attention that way.

- ▶ Make sure you deliver the "short form" of your presentation. Try to talk for less than 30 minutes, and no more than 45 minutes. After a meal, people don't want to stay seated for more time than that.

GETTING THE LAY OF THE LAND

No matter what size of room you are given, you'll want to walk the room and get comfortable with it. If possible, visit the place when nobody is there. Look around, stand on the stage, sit in a seat. Get a view from every angle. This little technique will go a long way in lowering your stress level before the presentation.

If you are prone to getting a dry mouth during a presentation, make sure there is water set up for you. Store the water on the podium, or on a table near the front of the room. That way, if you need it during the presentation, it will be easily accessible.

Giving a business presentation can actually be a lot of fun. Once you are prepared and have the lay of the land, you are ready to go.

In the next chapter I discuss how to give presentations across electronic media—via video conferencing and radio and television presentations.

10

Video Conferencing and Mass Media

Some day your business presentations could take you to far-off lands and unfamiliar places—without ever leaving home. With today's technology, that day could come sooner than you think. No, I'm not talking about "Star Trek" and beaming me up, Scottie. I am talking about using electronic media to transmit your message.

Video teleconferencing, satellite up-links and down-links, electronic chalkboards, and other technologies are poised to redefine the way people communicate with each other. With prices plummeting and technology expanding, long-distance and even overseas presentations are becoming more common.

This chapter introduces the fine art of delivering presentations over electronic media. Whether it's a video conference, an audio conference, or a televised event, you should know some of the ins and outs of making your presentations through a camera and microphone. I start with video conferencing, the latest trend. The technology isn't new, but its recent acceptance has changed the way some people think about giving presentations.

Next I cover more traditional mass media: radio and television. Although many business presenters will never venture into a studio, it's a good idea to know some of the tips and tricks, should the casting director call. You'll also find that preparing for a radio show is much like getting ready for an audio conference. Likewise, TV presentations are similar to video teleconferences. Whichever type of presentation you're tackling, knowing a few pointers will help you do your very best.

THE VIDEO CONFERENCE: KEEPING UP WITH THE JETSONS

The first picture phone was introduced in 1964 at the New York World's Fair. People assumed that in no time everyone would be communicating like George and Jane Jetson. That hasn't happened yet, but in the business world video communication is a reality.

The 1964 AT&T picture phone was costly and not at all practical. Transmission cost $1,000 a minute. Without today's digital compression technology, transmitting an analog TV image required the transmission capacity of 4,500 copper wire phone lines.

That picture phone went into someone's closet, but those who saw it never forgot it. Every new technology that has come along since then, from satellites to PCs and fiber optic cables, has paved a more practical way for the concept of video conferencing to actually fly.

While video phones are still too impractical for home use, businesses are beginning to embrace the technology. Some believe video conferencing will become as much a business necessity as the fax machine has. Only the next few years will tell.

Why Hold a Video Conference?

In a video conference, participants can not only see and hear one another, but they can interact using screen sharing (the screen displays the presentation along with an additional window in the corner of the screen for the person's close-up). It's almost as good as being there.

Video conferencing shows great promise for people who transact business from different places, from around the block to around the world. It could save on travel costs, it should save on labor costs, and— better yet—it may even let people change the way they do business.

How Does It Work?

Video conferencing combines television monitors and cameras, computers, special encoder/decoders called *codecs,* and digital transmission services from long-distance carriers. The majority of video conferencing systems require an ISDN (Integrated Services Digital Network) phone line, an all-digital (even for voice transmission) phone service that can carry 64K per second per line. No modem is needed. Regular phone lines, by contrast, transmit analog signals only (that's why you need the modem). ISDN service isn't available everywhere, but phone companies are busy laying cable and it is becoming more widespread.

Typically, a business presentation given via video conferencing incorporates the following components:

▶ One or more television cameras

▶ One or more speaker phones or headsets

▶ Cameras aimed at the people speaking

▶ Voice and video communications circuits activated at all participating locations

▶ A control system that allows setup and control access to participating locations

▶ An agenda and schedule for presentations and discussions by the video conferees—consisting of slide presentations, conference notes, and other materials prepared by the presenters and available to the other conferees attending the teleconference

Equipment and Costs

Equipment generally falls into one of two categories: video conference rooms and desktop video conferencing equipment. Because of technological advances such as video signal compression, the cost of codecs has gone down and video conferencing systems have dropped to an affordable price. Setting up a room typically costs about $20,000. For desktop video conferencing on a standard PC, the price can be as low as $2,000.

Besides the initial layout for equipment, there is a charge for transmission; vendors quote a rate of $15 to $30 an hour.

Adjusting Your Delivery

If you are called upon to deliver your presentation as part of a video conference, you'll have to learn some of the skills that TV broadcasters use.

Desktop video conferencing presents a few more challenges. You sit in front of a PC that has a camera and microphone (sometimes you must wear an earpiece with a special microphone attached, as shown in Figure 10-1). Then you have a face-to-face meeting with your audience.

Remember that presenting on a desktop system does have its limitations. The picture you (and the audience) see is strictly a head-and-shoulders shot at best, so making arm movements to emphasize your delivery is futile. Unless your arm and hand gestures are in front of your face, your audience won't see them.

Setting Up the Conference

Video conferencing programs are very much like television programs. Make sure you check the schedules, procedures, visuals, and agendas with the conference organizers. If it is your job to organize a conference, prepare a checklist for all participants. Rehearse with them. Check both their visuals and their appearance on camera. Give them plenty of time to prepare and make changes, if necessary.

During a video conference, you will probably be seated at a conference table, either by yourself or with others. You will either be participating in a conversation or have an allotted time to speak.

Each participant sits facing a camera; a monitor shows the people on the other end of the conference (see Figure 10-2). Sometimes there is a moderator who will introduce each speaker and coordinate the flow of the program.

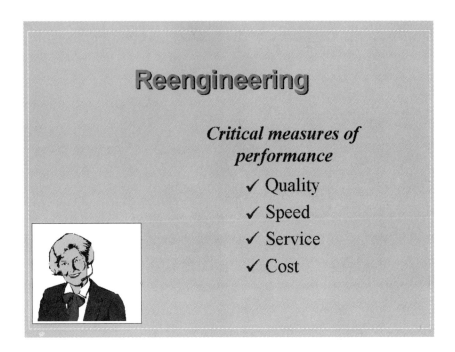

Figure 10–1   While you are giving a desktop video presentation on reengineering, your face appears in a corner of the screen. Wearing a headset with a microphone attached frees up your hands to control the computer and handle your notes.

If you have the equipment, dedicate a computer projection monitor and presentation software at the remote site. Download the graphic files prior to the meeting and have a presenter at the remote site cue the screen there.

Multiperson video conferences are usually located in a conference room or in a "quiet" area. The most important thing is to make sure there isn't a lot of background noise or traffic. If you are coordinating a conference, look for a private room in which to hold your conference. Minimize people's movements in and out of the room. (There's something about a video camera. Put one out and everyone wants to be a star.)

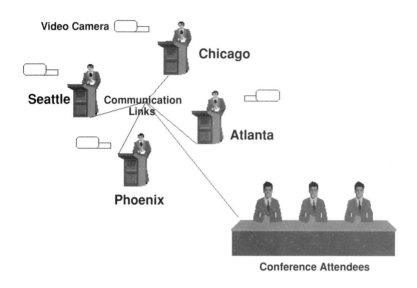

Figure 10–2 This is a sample layout of what a video conference
session with five connections would look like.

Let others in your office know you are having a conference and
ask them not disturb you. Remove all potential distractions, like tele-
phones and beepers, from the room.

If you are presenting with desktop video conferencing equipment,
you will probably do the presentation from your own desk or one that
has been set up with the conferencing equipment. In any case, you will
probably be seated rather than standing. On top of the computer
monitor, there will be a small camera focused on your face. The person
you are speaking to will see your face in a small window and your presentation on a larger window on their screen. Your colleague may even be
able to interact with your presentation and make comments on-the-fly.

Another technique, used by some long-distance learning centers
to minimize costs, is to have a single instructor whose image is transmitted to multiple sites. The audience can respond with questions on
separate audio channels that are displayed to the instructor.

Special Considerations

You'll find that speaking in a video conference does change a few of the standard presentation rules. To accommodate the equipment, you may have to learn how to make your presentation while seated rather than standing, you may have to adjust your clothing, and you may even need to change your timing.

In the following sections we'll discuss the most important adjustments that video conferences require.

Timing

Timing is very important. Pick out a key point that you want to address and concentrate on getting that point across. Stick to the agenda. Remember that the meeting planners must allot time segments to each presenter. Make sure you don't run over your allocated time and short-change your colleagues.

Wardrobe

Check the background color in the conference area before you select your presentation outfit. If the walls in the room are brown, don't wear brown. The audience won't be able to see you clearly. Wear colors that enhance rather than detract from your appearance. If in doubt, look at yourself on camera.

Dress simply. Women should not wear dangling or noisy jewelry. Men should not wear ties with loud patterns. The best colors are off-white or pastels without patterns. Avoid blouses or shirts made from shiny material that might reflect light toward the camera.

Delivery

Delivery for video conferencing is much like standard presentations, but with a twist. If the video signal is weak, there may be a time-delay in the video signal. Your voice and image may not be synchronized.

If you have never appeared on camera before, make time for rehearsal. In a video presentation, the camera becomes your focus. Make sure you treat the camera as your "audience." Pay attention to how you interact with others in the room with you. We'll discuss this in more detail in the section on TV presentation skills.

Always remember that the person on the other end of the camera cannot see everything in the conference room. Don't assume that they can or cannot see any part of your visuals—explain everything in detail.

Depending on the situation, it may be appropriate to interact with your audience on a periodic basis. Ask whether they understand what you've said and whether they have any questions. Answer the questions immediately rather than waiting until the end of the presentation. Always verify that the audience is "in sync" with you.

Keep the following things in mind:

▶ If the presentation is to be a discussion, look at the moderator instead of the camera.

▶ If someone else is talking, look at them, not the camera.

▶ Everything you do appears to be amplified in a video presentation. Be aware of this when waving your arms or gesturing toward the camera.

Video conferencing is a way for you to contact those who cannot break away from their busy schedules to make it to your presentation in person. It's a method to link up people worldwide. It may take a little more planning and coordination than a normal presentation, but the benefits outweigh the effort. You will be able to reach everyone, including those who can't come to you.

SPREADING YOUR MESSAGE THROUGH MASS MEDIA

The communication media of radio and television are decidedly different. The one similarity is that they are both forms of mass communication. One message (and one mistake) can reach a vast audience instantaneously. What you say, and how you say it, will be transmitted. There's no turning back.

There are additional skills required to make your point effectively when you appear in the media.

Radio: It's All in the Voice

Because radio is an audio medium, it doesn't matter what you do with you hands or the rest of your body when you speak. Keep in mind that you can make all kinds of emphatic gestures with your hands, fingers, head, and eyes—and they will all be meaningless. In this setting, your message lies strictly in your words and in your voice. Thus your inflection, how you pronounce and enunciate your words, how you build your phrases, and how you verbally create an image take on more importance than they would have in a typical audio-visual presentation.

Using Words to Create an Image

Years ago, a generation of young radio listeners found themselves enchanted by actor William Conrad. He was the original "masked man" who rode out of the Old West "on the thundering hooves of his great white horse, Silver." The Lone Ranger captured the national imagination.

It was the deep voice of Conrad that gave strength to the character. His voice made people believe that it would only take one shot to rid the world of another black-hatted outlaw. His voice made listeners know that he would win every fistfight, because his fists were like steel. Conrad's fans couldn't wait for the next episode. He and his effective voice would take them to the Old West with its mountains and valleys, the rivers and forests, the desert, the racing horses, and the exciting chases.

Then, both the Lone Ranger and William Conrad came to television—and both were disappointments. The televised Lone Ranger wasn't the character his fans remembered. William Conrad had the voice, but he did not measure up physically to the picture he had created in the listeners' minds. The wonder, awe, and mystery of the radio show proved to be false, and learning that reality hurt both the listeners and the sponsors. (It took an entirely different actor, Clayton Moore, to make the show popular again on TV.)

In a way, audio can be much more powerful than video. A voice by itself creates a special atmosphere, since the listeners make up the perfect visual image to go along with the audio. But if the voice doesn't move the audience, they lose interest. That's why it's so important to train your voice as the professionals do.

Training Your Voice

Take a newspaper article off to a quiet place. If you have a tape recorder, take that along. Read the article aloud. The object of this exercise is for you to hear how you sound, how you pronounce words, and how you pace phrases. Would anyone else want to listen to you the way you delivered that piece?

Every word and phrase in a newspaper article has a purpose, or it wouldn't be there. As you repeat the tape recorder exercise, try these techniques:

➤ Say each word and phrase with conviction.

➤ Don't race over any part of a word or a phrase.

➤ Use each word to set up the next, or to emphasize the previous one.

Now don't think that reading a newspaper is an appropriate way to prepare for being on the radio. The words and phrases and style are totally different. This exercise is simply for you to find out how you sound when you speak. If you are like most of us, you will play the tape back, listen to yourself for a moment, and want desperately to ram the tape down the garbage disposal.

Typically, people do not like the sound of their voices. They sound different than they thought they did. When you listen to a tape recording, you are faced with reality—like it or not.

If you are not comfortable with the sound of your voice, continue to practice over and over until you are comfortable. Does your voice sound scratchy or crack during your presentation experiment? Then try taking some deep breaths or a drink of water to help stabilize your voice and tape your presentation again. Or try to speed up, slow down, lower, or raise your voice. Keep recording your voice until you feel comfortable with the way you sound. Once you have confidence in the way you sound, you will feel comfortable presenting before large groups of people.

Television: Keeping Cool When All Eyes Are on You

Unlike radio, television requires no imagination on the part of the audience. They can see the actors or speakers and hear their voices; viewers don't have to do anything but watch.

What happens on the other side of the camera or microphone when you make a point on radio or television? On the radio it is a well-written script and skilled delivery that make a good presentation. But on television, the script, voice, face, and visuals all work together.

The television presentation is most similar to a presentation given in the conference room or banquet hall, in that you must be conscious of what you say, what you show, how you look, and how you present yourself. There is one major difference—the TV camera! Read on to find out how to use the camera to your advantage.

How do you look at a camera? You don't! Remember this as a general rule of thumb. There are situations where relating to the camera is necessary and expected, but, generally speaking, it is not a critical part of your presentation.

How you relate to the camera depends upon the situation. Are you alone with the camera or is the camera merely there to pick up your interaction with other members of a panel and a moderator? Or are you speaking to an audience?

When in fact you must deal with the camera, eye contact is just as important as it is in person-to-person speech—only you use a different technique. For TV, it is critical that you remember to look *through* the camera. Do not look at the camera itself as an object. If you do, it is very obvious to the viewing audience and you won't relate to them. You will look like an amateur.

Making Friends with the Camera

Imagine that on the other side of the camera is someone you know well and to whom you relate easily. Maybe it is your very best friend on the other side, or a spouse, lover, or friendly associate. Some experts advise that you "make love to the camera." In a sense, that is what you must do. It might be easier to think of the camera operator as either a good friend or new acquaintance that you like very much. You can tell the operator all about why you are excited about your topic. If you use that approach, you will project an image of an honest, warm, and sincere person.

Remember to look through the lens at the person you're picturing there. Pretend that you are discussing the subject and your recommendations with that friend.

The Panel Show Format

Some TV presentations are delivered in a panel-show format. If you are a part of a panel, usually there is a moderator and at least one or two other panel members. In this scenario, your attention is focused almost entirely on these people and not on the audience or the camera. It is usually the moderator that serves as your focal point. The moderator is the person who asks the questions and conducts the program.

In this scenario, there is rarely a need for you to look into the camera. One exception, which occurs at the beginning of the show, is the introduction of the guests. During the introduction, the camera is usually on you while the moderator gives the audience your name and the key points of your background. What do you do during these moments, when all of the attention is focused on you?

The easiest solution, and the one that always makes you look the most comfortable, is to continue to focus your eyes on the moderator and ignore the camera completely. Don't slouch in your chair. Maintain good posture, and let your face settle into a soft, gentle smile. Turn up the corners just a little bit. An ear-to-ear grin is not the answer.

Be yourself. If you show good posture (but not too stiff or straight) and a gentle smile, you'll appear friendly, pleasant, and confident, and the audience will look forward to hearing what you have to say.

Dressing for Success

What you wear is important for your on-camera presentation. Stay away from bright colors. Stark reds, whites, and blacks, don't work well, as a general rule. Wear more subtle colors. Avoid eye-grabbing plaids and stripes as well. Bold patterns can actually cause "video noise" that distorts the picture. (Look for this when you next watch TV; you'll be surprised when it appears.) Softer colors work best for both men and women. These colors allow the audience to focus on your face instead of your outfit.

For the same reason, steer clear of too much contrast in your clothing. For women, a soft white blouse and scarf work well, as long as the colors of the scarf blend with the suit.

A pale appearance can be problematic for some people. Professional studios use powder and makeup to cover the white faces of television personalities, attempting to cut down on the contrast between light and dark. The powder and makeup absorb more of the bright light, and work to reduce glare.

For men with this problem, a blue shirt is the best solution, with a tie that blends with both the shirt and suit. A white shirt tends to reflect the light and make your face appear too white. The blue shirt and dark suit help to minimize reflection.

People with darker skin tones don't have the problem of lights reflecting off their face. The camera sees a quieter, softer object. If you have dark skin tones, follow the same recommendations for your wardrobe, but a bit in reverse. You can wear a white shirt, but avoid too sharp a contrast with other clothing. Again, blue or another pastel-colored, button-down shirt is a good choice.

Facing the Bright Lights

Whenever you appear on television, the light is very bright and colors are intensified. That means that a white face, a white shirt, or white stripes on a tie will shine brilliantly, and can distract to the audience.

The lights are also very hot, and if you are going to be under them for a 30-minute show, you'll need to be conscious of their effect when choosing your clothing and makeup. Perspiration running through an inch of makeup creates an effect you'd probably rather avoid. Don't wear wool or other warm fabrics either. You can almost bet on perspiration, so be as prepared as you can.

Action on the Set

The television studio is a place like none other. It is usually a large room with a very high ceiling—and ugly. Generally, upon entering the studio you'll be surprised at how cool it is. This is a tip-off that when the lights go on, things warm up significantly.

Off in one corner is the "set," with the chairs and tables or counters, and most likely three, big cameras all pointing at that little set.

When the lights are turned on, everything is focused on the set. And if you are in that set, you feel as if you and the other person or persons there with you are the only people left in the whole world. The lights are really bright, and your first impulse will be to squint your eyes and want your sunglasses. Don't worry—you will adjust in only a few moments.

Outside that little set, there is usually a multitude of things going on. The camerapeople are moving about, the cameras themselves are moving about, the floor manager is going from person to person whispering, while the director of the show, sitting in the studio somewhere else, is talking to everyone over the headsets. With the director is a crew who look over all the camera shots, push buttons, load tapes and film, and otherwise take care of the technical side of things.

Throughout the show, you may hear the faint sound of someone talking. The director is constantly talking to the camerapeople, asking them to adjust their shot or move their camera to a new position for a totally different shot. The whispered responses you may hear are the camerapeople verifying their position or their shot.

The floor manager may give you hand signals or written instructions to alert you to how much time is left before the commercial break. You need to keep aware of these instructions without looking like you are distracted.

Keeping Your Focus

Concentration is key. You will have many distractions, but you must concentrate on what you are doing and saying. Pay no attention to anything that is happening outside that little circle of lights. Let the studio crew do whatever they have to do while you concentrate on what you have to do.

It is easy to get caught up in the activity around you. Chances are that you haven't been on TV before, and you feel excited about being in a television studio. This is why you really need to concentrate on your purpose for being there. Focus on your mission, your message, your knowledge, and your relationship and interaction with the others within the circle of lights.

Remember your posture. Whenever there is a commercial, straighten your tie or scarf, and make sure your suit coat is flat. Giving yourself something to do during these breaks helps relieve your tension and nervousness.

Keep your hands and arms in a comfortable position above the counter or desktop. Settle into a position where the use of your hands will be easy. Try not to wave your hands and arms too much for emphasis. Remember, the normal camera shot will show only your head and shoulders. Making gestures with your hands and arms off to the side will add nothing to what you are saying, but simple little movements just below the chin and slightly above the chest are very appropriate.

When another person on the show is speaking, look at that person. It is very distracting to the viewer, not to mention rude to the speaker, when you are looking around the room. It is very important to remember that the cameras could be focused on the person speaking, the entire set, or even on you.

We have all seen the panel show on television where one person obviously thinks that the camera is looking somewhere else, and this person is caught looking around and apparently not interested in the subject matter being discussed. Don't get caught!

In this section, I discussed developing your style and skill. I gave you pointers on how to make sure the room is just right, and also covered what to do to participate on a panel presentation, radio interview, or television presentation. If you have practiced, prepared, and previewed your presentation, you should do just fine.

In the next chapter, I discuss the follow-up to your presentation. I know, you thought you were all through, but it is very important to review and evaluate your presentation. Learning how to do a post-mortem on your performance will help you improve your next presentation.

IV

POSTMORTEM AND PUTTING IT ALL TOGETHER

When you finish delivering a business presentation, you may get a wonderful feeling of accomplishment. Whew, you're done! Right? Well, not really. Your presentation may indeed be over, but you aren't finished yet.

Business presentations are a means to an end, not an end in themselves. Most people have plenty of follow-up work to do even when the show is over. You may have more research to do, a new assignment, or even another presentation to plan for. In fact, depending on the type of presentation you've just made, your work could be just beginning.

In Chapter 11, I discuss some of the standard follow-up activities for business presentations. I also focus on how you can learn from your experience. Successful business presenters usually seek feedback not only to measure the effectiveness of their presentations, but to learn how to improve.

In Chapter 12, I give you an example of a real-life business presentation. I take it from start to finish and step through the paces, covering most of the techniques presented in the book.

Making It Easier Next Time

So far, the main focus of this book has been how to plan, prepare, and deliver business presentations. By now, you should have a good idea of how to get started. You've learned plenty of tips and techniques.

You may have already developed or refined a presentation using some of the ideas presented in this book—or perhaps you simply used the book as a guide to update a presentation you had already prepared.

What's next? The final step is to review your experience, analyze it, and make your presentation better the next time. The best lessons you'll learn come from trial and error.

This chapter covers some of the follow-up activities you should undertake after the presentation is over. I concentrate on how you should solicit feedback and analyze it so you know your strengths and weaknesses.

GETTING FEEDBACK

The best way to gauge the effectiveness of your presentation is to follow up with members of your audience. Get their opinions and perceptions about what you had to say and how well you delivered your message. Sometimes you can follow up by giving the audience an evaluation form to fill out.

Of course, in some business settings, such as a presentation to the budget approval committee, this technique is inappropriate. But you can still solicit feedback in other, less formal ways.

Using Questionnaires

Distribute evaluation forms immediately after the presentation, while ideas and comments are still fresh in the audience members' minds. Here are some recommended questions:

- ▶ What was the message you got from the presentation?
- ▶ What expectations did you have coming into the presentation?
- ▶ Did the presentation meet those expectations?
- ▶ Did you find the presentation interesting?
- ▶ Were the visuals helpful?
- ▶ Were the handouts helpful?
- ▶ Was the material that was presented too basic? Too technical? Just right?
- ▶ What other information would have been helpful?
- ▶ Did you find the presentation exciting?
- ▶ Did you find the presentation informative?
- ▶ Were there topics that I should have covered in more detail? Less detail?
- ▶ What was the best part of the presentation?
- ▶ What part(s) of the presentation need improvement? How should they be improved?

Table 11-1 Sample Evaluation Form

Presentation Element	Rating*				
Speaker					
Knowledge of topic	1	2	3	4	5
Style and delivery	1	2	3	4	5
Handling questions	1	2	3	4	5
Visuals					
Quality of content	1	2	3	4	5
Readability	1	2	3	4	5

*Rating scale: 5–Excellent, 4–Very Good, 3–Average, 2–Less than expected, 1–Poor

If you use an evaluation form, ask your audience to rate certain elements of the presentation on a scale from 1 to 5, for example:

Excellent	5
Very Good	4
Average	3
Less than expected	2
Poor	1

This point scale gives your audience an opportunity to tell you where you excelled, where your performance was average, and where you failed to meet their expectations. It is simple to follow.

As you create your evaluation form, make sure you place the rating numbers next to the evaluation criteria. Most people find it easier to circle numbers than to write them. This will make it easier on you, too. You won't have to try and decipher the handwriting, and as you flip through the evaluations, you'll see the trends almost as clearly as a graph. Table 11-1 gives a sample of categories you can ask the audience to rate.

Taking an Informal Survey

A friendly follow-up call to several members of your audience serves two purposes. First, you get advice about how to improve your presentation. Second, you establish better relationships with members of your audience. This works well in corporate and large organizational settings, especially when you solicit advice from senior managers.

Ask for honest feedback. If you feel the person is uncomfortable providing criticism, you might have to prime the response. For example, you can ask, "I felt like the cost-of-sales analysis was a little weak. Perhaps I could have added more information?" Or you could say, "I was concerned that I didn't cover the parking lot problem well enough. What do you think?"

Encourage criticism. While everyone likes to hear a kind word, don't look for praise. You won't learn as much from compliments as you will from criticisms.

Don't expect to get a complete picture from your informal phone calls. Most likely, people will be more comfortable about criticizing your content than your style.

Observing the Audience

During a speech to a large audience you may not be able to survey your audience. Sometimes you'll just have to evaluate your presentation based on the audience response. To do your own evaluation, try to tune into the response from your audience. Look around the room to see how they react during the delivery of your speech. Here are a few questions you can ask yourself:

▶ Do you hear talking going on during your presentation or do you have a captive audience?

▶ Do people get up and leave while you're speaking or are you presenting enough interesting information to keep them in their seats?

▶ Did the audience appreciate your jokes and humor or did you make them feel uncomfortable?

▶ Was there a time when you felt you lost your audience? If so, what can you do to correct that?

If you have paper notes, use them during your speech to keep score. Mark an ✕ by the section that got bad responses and a ✓ by the ones that left a very positive response.

How Did You Rate?

Track the information you receive. Note how many people gave you feedback, either verbally or through your evaluation form. Look at their responses for trends. Was the general feeling favorable? Were there parts of the presentation that you could improve?

Evaluating Your Strengths and Weaknesses

Keeping your ratings and evaluation forms is important. Over time, as you continue to give more business presentations, you'll develop a good sense of what you do right and what your problem areas are.

You may find that you do better with some topics than with others. You may also discover that using certain types of visuals helps boost your scores. Perhaps you will spot a trend in how you appeal to different types of audiences. Are you better received by a technical audience than one filled with executives? Why? Is it your appearance or your use of overly technical jargon?

As you develop a database of scores, you can begin to look for ways to improve. You may find that certain techniques work for some audiences and not for others.

Planning for the Next Time

All the data you gather will be useful the next time you plan a presentation. You can make changes if the audience felt something needed work. If a certain portion of the presentation was received very favorably, make sure you do it again.

FINDING YOUR OWN WAY

All the sophisticated software and presentation aids in the world can't take your place. As a speaker, you are going to have to find your own style and become comfortable with it. You must have something meaningful to say and know what you are talking about. You must also believe in what you say and be confident in how you say it.

Learning how to speak is the single most effective thing you can do to further your career, next to knowing how to express yourself in writing. Good speakers are perceived as good thinkers and leaders. Many highly successful people are persuasive presenters.

Remember, the chance to speak in front of an audience is a privilege. It is an opportunity to share your thoughts, ideas, and dreams with a receptive audience. Give it all that you have, and more. If you do this well, you will be successful and you will open a vast range of other opportunities for yourself.

You'll be a great success when you learn to combine content, style, and form. While practice alone doesn't make perfect, practice combined with review, analysis, and use of the right techniques will undoubtedly make you a great presenter.

In this chapter, I covered the standard follow-up activities and described what you should do with the feedback or evaluations by others. I discussed how you can evaluate your own presentation, then use this information to analyze your presentation and improve it for the next time. Now, let's do a sample presentation together. In the next chapter I put these techniques to work.

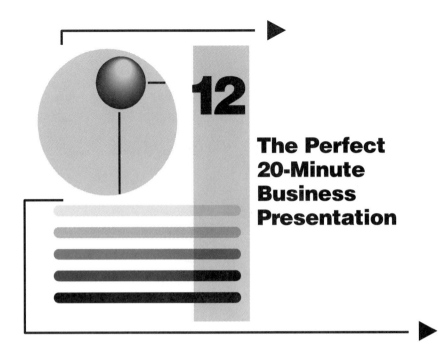

The Perfect 20-Minute Business Presentation

Here's your assignment: You just received a call from your organization's newly appointed chief operating officer. He has spent time reviewing the organization and is concerned that the company is not using information technology effectively. He feels that the company's technology is decades behind others in the industry. He asks you to prepare a short presentation about where technology is going and what opportunities you see for the organization to make better use of it. You need to provide a high-level overview with a few specific recommendations.

Following the format for putting a plan together from Chapter 2, you can begin to assemble your game plan.

THE FIVE W'S

Remember "the five W's" I talked about in Chapter 2? Begin with them to gather some pertinent facts about your presentation: *what, why, who, when,* and *where.*

What

- ▶ What are you supposed to be speaking about?
- ▶ What is the topic, and what kind of message about that topic will you deliver?

In this case, your topic is "trends in information technology." You must deliver a presentation about these trends and how they affect the organization's business.

Why

- ▶ Why are you giving this presentation?
- ▶ Do you need to persuade, inform, or update the audience?
- ▶ Are you trying to get them to take action? Will you be presenting good news or bad?

In our example, your purpose is partly to inform and partly to sell. You need to tell your audience what's going on, but you also want to encourage them to act. The news you likely present will be both good and bad. The bad news is that the company doesn't use technology wisely. The good news is that there's hope: If the managers (your audience) act on your recommendations, the organization can redeem itself.

An important part of your mission is to get the audience to do something. You want them to take the next steps and explore the opportunities.

Who

- ▶ Who are the members of your audience?
- ▶ What do they know now?
- ▶ Do they have any preconceived notions about your topic?
- ▶ How many people are expected to attend?

In this example, your audience consists of the senior management team. You're making your presentation to the vice presidents in charge of sales, order fulfillment, manufacturing, and human resources—as well as the chief financial officer, chief operating officer, and chief executive officer. With the exception of the COO, most of the audience members are not well-versed in technology.

While the organization seems to have a lot of computers, most of the executives don't use them personally. The company has spent a lot of money on technology over the past few years, but has little to show for it. Most of the executives are biased against technology. (In fact, you doubt that any of them could program their own VCRs—even with a well-written manual!)

Considering this information about your audience, you would definitely want to make the executives feel comfortable with the knowledge that they do have. You would not want to talk down to them, but reassure them that they want to keep up with their competitors. Be more specific in what technology can do for them, how it can help the company, or save money and time down the road.

When

- ▶ What is the presentation day, date, and time?
- ▶ Who is speaking before you?
- ▶ How much time do you have?
- ▶ Can the audience ask questions?
- ▶ Is this a mealtime event where you will have to compete with clinking dishes and cups?

Your presentation is scheduled for three weeks from now, on a Tuesday at 4 p.m. You have a half-hour time slot, but should only talk for 20 minutes. You should save the last 10 minutes for questions and answers. No one is to give a speech before you do, but the chief operation officer will introduce you and tell the audience why he asked you to speak to them about this topic. There are to be no refreshments other than coffee.

Where

▶ Will you speak in a cramped conference room or an exotic ballroom?

▶ What audiovisual equipment will be available to you?

▶ How about the room lighting: Is it adjustable if you choose to bring in computer-driven visuals?

You're delivering your presentation in the executive conference room. The room is filled with audiovisual equipment, so you shouldn't have a problem getting any presentation aid you want. The room offers you excellent control of lighting, so you don't have to worry about your visuals being difficult to see.

The room is long and narrow, and there's ample space in front for your AV equipment. There is a podium off to one side, as well as a rolling table that can be pulled into the front of the room. If you want, you can set up a dual projection system that lets you view your visuals on a screen in front of you, while the audience views another image behind you.

Luckily, you have a chance to go to the conference room well in advance of the meeting. In fact, you can book the conference room from noon until 5 p.m. on the day of the presentation. So you have plenty of time to set up.

14 STEPS TO PRESENTATION SUCCESS

Sketch out a schedule and plan of action. Table 12-1 lists the 14 key steps to making a quality presentation. Check off each one as you complete it

MAKING IT HAPPEN!

The challenge is now yours. You have all the materials you need to develop and research the next presentation. You know what you want

Table 12–1 Fourteen Key Steps to Making a Presentation

Task	Status
1. **Develop the presentation plan**—answering the five W's	Already done; much of the information supplied by COO
2. **Develop an outline**—what is your message, your mission?	Use PowerPoint to outline key points and supporting arguments
3. **Research the facts**—adding third-party source content	Use on-line services, CompuServe's access to the CompDB database, and Dow Jones News Retrieval
4. **Set up design for visuals**—choosing basics of colors, font, and layout	Use standard template(s) from PowerPoint (like blue background, white titles, yellow text)
5. **Develop a storyboard**—setting up your visuals	Use PowerPoint's slide sorter feature
6. **Produce samples**—printing out visuals (both color and b/w)	Use laser-jet printer for b/w visuals and thermal printer for color
7. **Get approvals**—testing with pilot audience, the boss, or others	Schedule meeting with COO about 7–10 days before the presentation
8. **Pilot and rehearse**—running through your presentation	Practice in front of a video camera and have others evaluate your presentation
9. **Revise storyboard, visuals, etc.**—responding to the evaluations you get	Change wording and examples based on feedback of those who saw preview
10. **Produce visuals**—if applicable	Since visuals will be presented on-screen, you don't have to produce slides or overheads
11. **Produce handouts**—giving supporting data in a handout	Make color covers on thermal printer, high-resolution b/w copies on laser printer
12. **Time rehearsals**—does your speech fit the time allotted?	Check timing and flow; prepare last-minute notes
13. **Inspect the presentation room**—testing equipment, lights, etc.	Visit conference room two weeks before presentation; take computer and hook up AV equipment to make sure everything is compatible
14. **Step through final rehearsal**—using lights, equipment, and visuals	Reserve time in conference room a few days before; go through presentation and visualize success

to say and how you want to say it. You have practiced listening to your voice on tape, and you've seen yourself on video. You now know what to do with your hands, where to stand, and how to leave the stage.

Whether you are presenting to your boss and want approval for the most important project of your life, or you are addressing 5,000 colleagues at an industry conference—you want to share what's inside your head. Follow the guidelines presented in this book, then go out and make your point!

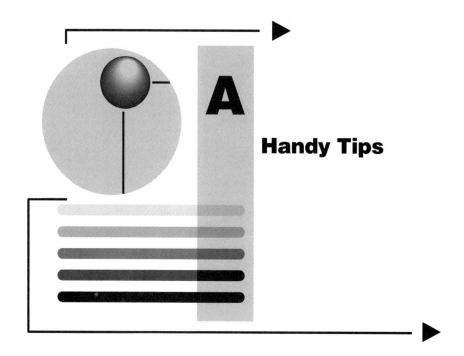

A
Handy Tips

Although each of the areas in this appendix is covered in depth elsewhere in this book, here they are summarized for your quick reference. These are the most helpful tips you can use to improve the way you plan and prepare your presentation, design your visuals, and deliver your talk.

PLANNING AND PREPARATION

The secret here is to organize fully, research wisely, and avoid jargon. This way you can be confident that your audience understands your talk at all times.

Organize, Organize

You cannot "over-organize" a presentation. Remember, you have just a few minutes to capture the interest and attention of your audience. Make it easy for them.

A good approach is to identify your major points early in the presentation, then refer back to them. It's like the old advice for a three-step presentation:

1. Tell them what you are going to tell them.
2. Tell them.
3. Tell them what you told them.

It's also important to summarize your key points into a few topic areas. Since most people will only retain three key points, make sure your message doesn't include too many key issues. You don't want to confuse your audience.

Many business presentations have an "action required" portion, where you want the audience to do something after the presentation. Figure out what you want them to do, then make sure you let them know it. If you want them to buy something, ask for the order. If you want them to tell all their friends about something, then suggest just that. Make no bones and never assume that people will figure out (or derive) the message from what you've told them.

Research Wisely

With today's easy access to information, you have little excuse for not knowing the pertinent facts of your subject material. Use all the available CD and on-line databases to gather your facts and defend your argument.

A well-rounded presentation gives several views of a topic. If time permits, introduce opposing points of views, then explain why your point of view is more valid.

Avoid Unexplained Jargon and Acronyms

Unless you know your audience very well, don't risk insulting them with technical jargon or acronyms. Do not assume that they read everything that you do, or that they have committed to memory the alphabet soup of acronyms that float about every industry.

If you think that most people in your audience know an acronym, then use it; but identify it later in a sentence. For example, if you are talking to a technical audience about MIPS (pronounced "mips") ratings, you could say:

Look at the change! Only 20 years ago, a MIPS cost $800,000. Today you can buy a personal computer for your kids that provides that unit of computing power—a million instructions per second—for about $20.

In this case, you've told the audience what a MIPS is (a unit of computing power) and spelled out the acronym (a million instructions per second).

CREATING YOUR VISUALS

Presenting visuals in an effective manner takes patience and practice. Keeping things simple can only help you.

Less Is Best

No matter what you put on your visual—text, art, or color—remember that less is best. Choose the simplest art and the fewest words, typefaces, and colors for each visual.

Avoid Font Follies

Most presentation software lets you choose from a wide variety of typefaces. In fact, the selection is so great that new presenters often use too many fonts. Avoid this temptation.

Try to select no more than two type styles per visual, and keep them consistent throughout your presentation. For example, if you select a serif typeface for a heading, use a sans serif typeface for the main points and sub-points.

Try out your font selection and make sure your charts are readable from a distance. Your audience shouldn't have to squint just to see them. (Review Chapter 5 for information about fonts.)

Use Color to Your Advantage

Color clarifies, so it can be used to highlight points, such as "Please pay the amount shown in red." Some organizations even believe that printing instructions in color can reduce the number of service and support calls, because people grasp the information more readily.

But don't throw color into your visuals indiscriminately. Learn about color. At the bookstore you'll find books on creating business presentations or newsletters that include chapters on colors. By reading these documents, you'll learn from the experts about which color combinations work and which ones don't work.

Believe it or not, people interpret colors quite differently. Some standards may be easy to figure out—like using red for stop, green for go, and yellow for caution. But make sure you understand how different cultures react to colors. For example, in certain cultures white is the color of mourning, and red is revolutionary. Be aware of cultural differences if you take your presentation to other countries.

Using too many colors (like using too many fonts or too many words) will confuse your readers. In the text portion of your documents, color should be used sparingly and only to highlight words or sentences. Color to the reader is like noise to the listener: Don't send out too many blaring messages or the audience will tune out your text.

Follow Standards and Templates

Once you develop a style that works for you, develop a few standards and create templates, or use the preformatted templates that come with your presentation software.

These standards are important, especially if you are new to using technology. You can jump quickly over the hurdles of adopting new technology if you settle down to using a few good templates.

IMPROVING YOUR STYLE AND DELIVERY

Your appearance affects how others think of you. If you stand before an audience and slouch, or nervously shift from side to side, your audience will undoubtedly pick up the feeling that you are uncomfortable. They may think you are unsure of your topic or that you have something to hide. If your body language is poor, or your gestures don't communicate a confident attitude, then your audience may spend more time looking at you than listening to you. Here are some suggestions to improve your style and delivery.

Learn the "Balanced Stance"

Inexperienced presenters often lose their balance when they get nervous. They shift their weight from one hip to the other, they cross their feet, and they distract their audience with all of this movement.

Speech coaches advise that you learn how to stand with your weight evenly distributed on both feet. To practice, stand tall with your feet facing forward, firmly planted. It helps to separate your feet by a few inches and gain your balance by relaxing and slightly bending your knees. You should lock into this position until you are ready to move. When you do move, take a few steps and then lock into a new standing position.

You may find it uncomfortable to talk and walk at the same time. If you do, simply take a few steps while you are advancing to the next visual.

Find a Place for Your Hands

Many new business presenters wonder what to do with their hands. They don't know when to use them and when to leave them alone. Sometimes they'll give an entire presentation with their elbows locked in place.

Try this: Stand tall and drop your hands to your sides. Hold them there for a few moments and then make hand gestures naturally. Consider your sides as the "home" position, so when you are finished making a gesture, just drop your hands to your sides.

If you are concerned about how to handle your hands, practice in front of a video recorder. Chances are, you'll be surprised how quickly you can develop a good speaking style when you see what you are doing right—and what you are doing wrong.

Practice Perfect Posture

Make a habit of standing tall and walking tall. A tip from professional models: stand flush with a wall. Align your shoulders, back, legs, and feet. See how straight you are? Now take one step away from the wall and try to maintain that straight back.

Breathe

Learn some breathing exercises. They will help you relax and speak more forcefully. Many people who don't like their voices actually cut off some of their air intake by not breathing correctly.

Listen to yourself on a tape recorder or video yourself. Watch and listen carefully. If you do not like what you see and hear, consider getting some professional coaching on proper breathing and posture.

Stand When You Speak

If you are giving an informal presentation, you might feel that you can stay seated while delivering your presentation. Don't.

Your voice will sound better when you stand, because you can speak from the diaphragm. To see this for yourself, tape-record your voice while seated. Then do it again when you are standing. No doubt you'll hear the difference in your voice.

Standing also helps when you want to take control of a telephone conversation. Your voice will come across more clearly if you stand—and, of course, the other party needn't know that you are not sitting down!

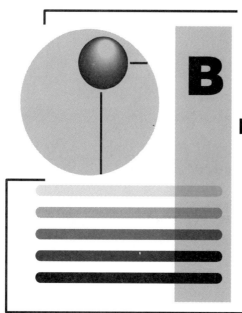

Resources

Access Softek 2550
9th Street, Suite 206
Berkeley, CA 94710
(510) 848-0606
SoundTrack, SoundTrack
CD-ROM

Acer America Corporation
2641 Orchard Parkway
San Jose, CA 95134
(408) 433-3636
Pentium multimedia computer

Ad Lib, Inc.
220 Grande-Allee Est., Suite 850
Quebec, Canada G1R 2J1
(800) 463-2686
Ad Lib Gold sound card

AimTech Corporation
20 Trafalgar Square
Nashua, NH 03063-1973
(603) 883-0220
IconAuthor

Aldus Corporation
411 First Avenue South
Seattle, WA 98104-2871
(206) 622-5500
Persuasion, FreeHand

America Online, Inc.
8619 Westwood Center Drive
Vienna, VA 22182-2285
(703) 448-8700
On-line service

Asymetrix
110 110th Avenue, Suite 700
Bellevue, WA 98004
(206) 462-0501
Multimedia ToolBook, Compel,
MediaBlitz, Splice

ATI Technologies
33 Commerce Valley Drive E
Thornhill, Ontario Canada
L3T 7N6
(905) 882-2600
MediaMerge, Graphics Ultra Pro,
Graphics Wonder, VIDEO-IT!

Autodesk, Inc.
2320 Marinship Way
Sausalito, CA 94965
(415) 332-2344
Animator Pro, 3D Studio

Barco
1552 E. Adams Park Drive
Covina, CA 91724
(818) 339-4042
Projector systems

Canon USA Inc.
One Canon Plaza
Lake Success, NY 11042-1113
(516) 488-6700
Printers

Big Noise Software, Inc.
P.O. Box 23740
Jacksonville, FL 32241
(904) 730-0754
Cadenza

ColorBytes
2525 S. Wadsworth Boulevard
Suite 308
Denver, CO 80227
(303) 989-9205
Stock photography CD-ROMs

Compaq Computer Corporation
20555 SH 249
Houston, TX 77070-2698
(800) 888-5858
Contura 400, Presario 900/920
Multimedia Computer

CompuServe
5000 Arlington Centre Blvd.
P.O. Box 20212
Columbus, OH 43220
(800) 848-8990
On-line service

Computer Support Corporation
15962 Midway Road
Dallas, TX 75244
(214) 661-8960
Arts & Letters

Consumer Technology
Northwest Inc.
7853 S.W. Cirrus Drive
Beaverton, OR 97008
(800) 356-3983
VGA–NTSC adapters

Corel Corporation
1600 Carling Avenue
Ottawa, Ontario, Canada
K1Z 8R7
(613) 728-8200
*CorelDRAW!, CorelPHOTO-
PAINT!, CorelMOVE!,
CorelSHOW!*

Creative Labs, Inc.
1901 McCarthy Boulevard
Milpitas, CA 95035
(408) 428-6600
SoundBlaster sound cards

CrystalGraphics
3110 Patrick Henry Drive
Santa Clara, CA 95054
(408) 496-6175
*Flying Fonts!, 3D Designer,
TOPAS*

DeltaPoint Software, Inc.2
Harris Court, Suite B-1
Monterey, CA 93940
(408) 648-4000
DeltaGraph

Doceo Publishing, Inc.
One Meca Way
Norcross, GA 30093
(404) 564-5545
Video compression sampler

Epson America, Inc.
20700 Madrona Avenue
Torrance, CA 90509-2842
(310) 782-4380
*Epson ActionTower 3000
multimedia computer, Epson ES-
800C scanner*

Farcast
1010 El Camino, Suite 300
Menlo Park, CA 94025
(415) 327-2446
News service

Fargo Electronics Inc.
NW 8279
P.O. Box 1450
Minneapolis, MN 55485-8279
(612) 941-3366
Primera color printer

Fractal Design Corporation
335 Spreckels Drive
Aptos, CA 95003
(408) 688-8800
Fractal Design Painter

Gale Research, Inc.
835 Penobscot Bldg.
Detroit, MI 48226
(313) 961-2242
The Gale Directory of Databases

General Magic, Inc.
2465 Latham Street, Suite 100
Mountain View, CA 94040
(415) 965-0400
Telescript agent technology

Gold Disk, Inc.
P.O. Box 789 Streetsville
Mississauga, Ontario, Canada
L5M 2C2
(416) 602-4000
Astound, Animation Works
Interactive

Gryphon Software Corporation
7220 Trade Street, Suite 120
San Diego, CA 92121
(619) 536-8815
Morph

Gyration Inc.
12930 Saratoga Avenue, #C6
Saratoga, CA 95070
(408) 255-3016
GyroPoint Remote

Hewlett-Packard
P.O. Box 1754
Greeley, CO 80632
(800) 752-0900
ScanJet Iicx scanner, HP Deskjet
color printers

HSC Software
1661 Lincoln Boulevard,
Suite 101
Santa Monica, CA 90404
(310) 392-8441
HSC InterActive

HyperMedia Communications
901 Mariner's Island Boulevard
Suite 365
San Mateo, CA 94404
(415) 573-5170
NewMedia magazine

Jandel Scientific Inc.
2591 Kerner Boulevard
San Rafael, CA 94901
(415) 453-6700
SigmaPlot

Image-In, Inc.
406 East 79th Street
Minneapolis, MN 55420
(800) 345-3540
Image-In Color, Image-In
Professional

Imagetects
P.O. Box 4
Saratoga, CA 95071
(408) 252-5487
Clip art CD-ROMs

IN:SYNC
7315 Wisconsin Avenue
Bethesda, MD 20814
(301) 831-5008
Razor software

Individual, Inc.
84 Sherman Street
Cambridge, MA 02140
(617) 354-2230
First!

InFocus Systems
27700B S.W. Parkway Avenue
Wilsonville, OR 97070
(503) 685-8888
LitePro, LCD projection systems

Integrated Media, Inc.
P.O. Box 55400
Boulder, CO 80322
(800) 274-5116
Publish! magazine

Intel Corporation
5200 N.E. Elam Young Way
Hillsboro, OR 97124-6497
(503) 629-8080
ProShare, Indeo

Lenel Systems International, Inc.
290 Woodcliff Office Park
Fairport, NY 14450
(716) 248-9720
MediaOrganizer, MediaDeveloper

Lotus Development Corporation
55 Cambridge, MA 02142
(617) 577-8500
Freelance Graphics, SmartPics

Macromedia
600 Townsend Street
Suite 310W
San Francisco, CA 94103
(415) 252-2000
*Action! CD-ROM for Windows,
Authorware, Director*

Masterclips Inc.
5201 Ravenswood Road
Suite 111
Fort Lauderdale, FL 33312
(305) 983-7440
Clip art libraries

Mathematica, Inc.
402 South Kentucky Avenue
Lakeland, FL 33801
(813) 682-1128
Tempra Pro

Media-Pedia Video Clips, Inc.
22 Fisher Avenue
Wellesley, MA 02181
(617) 235-5617
Media-Pedia video clips

Media Vision, Inc.
47221 Fremont Boulevard
Fremont, CA 94538
(510) 770-8600
Pro AudioSpectrum sound cards

Metatec Discovery Systems
7001 Discovery Boulevard
Dublin, OH 43017
(800) 637-3472
Nautilus CD-ROM

MicroCal Software Inc.
22 Industrial Drive
East Northampton, MA 01060
(800) 969-7720
Origin

Micrografx, Inc.
1303 East Arapaho Road
Richardson, TX 75081
(800) 733-3729
Charisma, Designer

Microsoft Corporation
One Microsoft Way
Redmond, WA 98052-6399
(800) 426-9400
Video for Windows, PowerPoint,
Word for Windows

Mind Path Technologies
12700 Park Central Drive
Suite 1707
Dallas, TX 75251
(214) 233-9296
Mind Path Presentation F/X

Mirus Industries Corporation
758 Sycamore Drive
Milpitas, CA 95035
(408) 944-9770
FilmPrinter film recorder

Mitsubishi Electronics America
5665 Plaza Drive
Cypress, CA 90630
(714) 220-2500
Computer monitors

Montage Publishing, Inc.
701 Westchester Avenue
White Plains, NY 10604
(914) 328-9157
AV Video

Multimedia Computing Corp.
3501 Ryder Street
Santa Clara, CA 95051
(408) 737-7575
Multimedia computing and
presentations

NEC Technologies, Inc.
1414 Massachusetts Avenue
Boxborough, MA 01729
(508) 264-8000
NEC Versa/V and Versa/M laptop
computers, computer monitors

New Media Corporation
One Technology
Irvine, CA 92718
(714) 453-0100
Peripherals

nView Corporation
860 Omni Blvd.
Newport News, VA 23606
(804) 873-1354
LCD projection monitors

Passport Designs, Inc.
625 Miramontes Street
Half Moon Bay, CA 94019
(415) 726-0280
Media Music, Trax

Paul Mace Software
400 Williamson Way
Ashland, OR 97520
(800) 523-0258
GRasp

PennWell Publishing Company
P.O. Box 3188
Tulsa, OK 74101
(918) 831-9423
Computer Artist, Computer
Graphics World

Polaroid Corporation
575 Technology Square
Cambridge, MA 02139
(617) 577-2000
Desktop film recorders

Prodigy Services Co.
445 Hamilton Avenue
White Plains, NY 10601
(914) 993-8000
On-line service

Prosonus
11126 Weddington Street
North Hollywood, CA 91601
(800) 999-6191
MusicBytes

Proxim
295 North Bernardo Avenue
Mountain View, CA 94043
(415) 960-1630
Peripherals

Qlogic Corporation
3545 Harbor Blvd.
Costa Mesa, CA 92626
(800) 867-7274
Peripherals

Reveal Computer Products
6045 Variel Avenue
Woodland Hills, CA 91367
(818) 594-8496
Memory, Hard Drives

Ron Scott, Inc.
1000 Jackson Boulevard
Houston, TX 77006
(713) 529-5868
HiRes QFX

Sense Interactive Corporation
1412 West Alabama Street
Houston, TX 77006
(713) 523-5757
Stock photography CD-ROMs

Shapeware Corporation
520 Pike Street, Suite 1800
Seattle, WA 98101-4001
(206) 521-4500
Visio

Sharp Electronics Corporation
Sharp Plaza
Mahwah, NJ 07430-2135
(201) 529-9500
LCD projection panels, computer monitors

Software Publishing Corporation
1901 Landings Drive
Mountain View, CA 94043
(408) 986-8000
Harvard Graphics, Harvard Spotlight

Sony Electronics Inc.
3300 Zanker Road
San Jose, CA 95134
(800) 352-7669
Computer monitors

Tektronix Graphics Printing
& Imaging
26600 S.W. Parkway Avenue
Wilsonville Industrial Park
Wilsonville, OR 97070
(503) 627-7111
Printers

Texas Instruments
13500 N. Central Expressway
Dallas, TX 75265
(214) 995-4360
TravelMate 4000, printers

Time Arts, Inc.
1425 Corporate Center Parkway
Santa Rosa, CA 95407
(707) 576-7722
Lumena

Traveling Software
18702 North Creek Parkway
Bothell, WA 98011
(206) 483-8088
LapLink Wireless Software

Turtle Beach Systems
1600 Pennsylvania Avenue
York, PA 17404
(717) 843-6916
Wave for Windows

Twelve Tone Systems
44 Pleasant Street
Watertown, MA 02172
(617) 926-2480
Cakewalk

VideoLabs, Inc.
5270 West 84th Street
Minneapolis, MN 55437
(612) 897-1995
VideoCam

Voyetra Technologies
333 Fifth Avenue
Pelham, NY 10803
(914) 738-4500
MusiClips

WordPerfect Corporation
1555 N. Technology Way
Orem, Utah 84057
(800)-321-0034
WordPerfect Presentations

Xircom
26025 Mureau Road
Calabasas, CA 91302
(818) 878-7600
PCMCIA peripherals

Zenith Data Systems
2150 East Lake Cook Road
Buffalo Grove, IL 60089
(708) 808-4497
Znote Laptop Computer

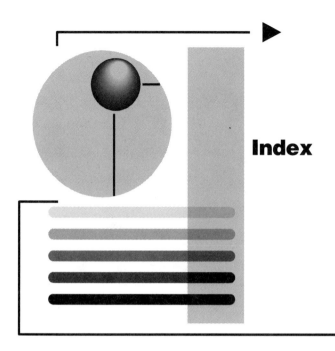

Index

A

Acronyms, defining, 31, 192–93

Action verbs as preferred in presentations, 32

Action! (Macromedia), 121–22
  Action Tool, Sound Tool, and Linking Tool of, 121

Active voice as preferred in presentations, 32

Ad libbing, resisting temptation to use, 141

Adrenaline, effects of, 139

Agent technology, 50–51

Alabama Resource Center, 113

Alignment of text for presentations, 68–70

America Online service, 51–52

downloading Video for Windows using, 118

Animation file formats importable to Action!, 121

Animation in presentations, presentation software features for, 95

Appearance of presenter, checklist for, 146–47

Approvals for presentation, 17

Assignment for a speaking presentation
  accepting, 12–14
  declining, 13

Astound (Gold Disk)
  features and best uses for, 97–98, 125–26

Bruskin, R.H., study of fear of
public speaking by, 5
Bulleted lists
alignment of text on left for,
68–69
consistent style of wording at
beginning of all items of,
64
continued to subsequent pages,
65
displayed one item at a time,
95
levels in, 65
rules for getting maximum
effect from, 64–65
word-processing programs to
prepare, 83
Bullets for lists
choosing special character for,
61–62
effects in presentation of
various, table listing, 63
limiting number of, 64
"Butterflies" in stomach, 138

C

Call for action in closing, 40
Camera
making friends with, 172
relating to, 171
Capital letters, refraining from
use of all, 66, 70–71
Caray, Harry, 138
CD-ROM
magazines available on, 48

number of titles in circulation
on, 48
for research, 47
CD-ROM drive
dual- or quad-speed, 119
external, 120
in laptop or notebook
computer, 120
multimedia presentations run
on, 115
Change over period of time, bar
and column charts to show,
77
Charisma (Micrografx, Inc.)
adding layers of objects and
effects using, 94–95
features and best uses for, 97
graphics features of, 92
system resources used by, 103
Charting tools, 99
Charts, 75–80, 86. *See also
individual types*
imported into presentation
software, 89–91
Clip art
to add life to presentation, 99
for bullets, 62
pacing presentation rate for, 80
Clip art libraries, 99–101, 103
Clipping services, electronic,
49–50
Clock wipe, 128
Closing of a presentation, 39–40
final goals covered in, 39
importance of good, 33

Video for Windows (Microsoft),
117
downloading, 118
Video phones, 162
Video recorders (camcorders) to
practice
to cultivate a speaker's voice,
144
trying different styles using,
142
using rented, 41
Video requirements for
presentation software, 104
Visio (Shapeware Corporation),
99–100
Visualizing a successful
presentation, 41
Visuals
as aid to comprehension, 4
avoiding distractions from, 159
bad, effects of, 57
designing, 57–82, 193–94
developing, 17
evaluating success of, 183
limiting amount of text on, 64
producing final, 17
revising, 17
wireless remote device to
control, 156
Voice
cultivating your speaker's,
144–45
trained for radio presentation,
170–71

W

Wardrobe for presenters. *See*
Clothes
Warm colors, 72–73
Water set up for speaker, 160
Wave Jammer (New Media
Corporation), 120
Whiteboard to handle audience
input, 155
Windows. *See* Microsoft
Windows
WingDings typeface of symbols
in Windows 3.1, chart of,
62
Wipes in multimedia
presentations, 128
Wodaski, Ron, five key areas to
producing video according
to, 127
Word recognition, 71
WordPerfect, 28
Word-processing software,
28–29, 83
Words
to create images during radio
presentation, 169–70
using short, effective, 31–32
using transition, 144–45

Prices of Selected Books from Prima Publishing

Computing Strategies for Reengineering Your Organization	$24.95
Reengineering ToolKit: Tools and Technologies for Reengineering Your Organization	$24.95
Software: What's Hot! What's Not!	$16.95
The CD-ROM Revolution	$24.95
Leadership and the Computer	$14.95
Better Speeches in Ten Simple Steps	$9.95
Speaker's and Toastmaster's Handbook	$14.95
How to Sell More Than 75 Percent of Your Freelance Writing, 2nd Edition	$12.95
How to Become a Successful Consultant in Your Own Field, 3rd Edition	$12.95

To order by phone with Visa or MasterCard, call (916) 632-4400, Monday–Friday, 9 a.m.– 5 p.m. Pacific Standard Time.

To order by mail fill out the information below and send with your remittance to: Prima Publishing, P.O. Box 1260, Rocklin, CA 95677-1260

Quantity	Title	Unit Price	Total
_____	_____	_____	_____
_____	_____	_____	_____
_____	_____	_____	_____
_____	_____	_____	_____
_____	_____	_____	_____

	_____
Subtotal	_____
7.25% Sales Tax (CA only)	_____
Shipping*	_____
Total	_____

Name _____

Street Address _____

City _____ State _____ ZIP _____

Visa/MC No. _____ Expires _____

Signature _____

*$4.00 shipping charge for the first book and 50¢ for each additional book.